meditation

exploring a great spiritual practice

meditation

Richard W. Chilson

John Kirvan, series editor

SORIN BOOKS™   Notre Dame, Indiana

www.avemariapress.com

International Standard Book Number: 1-893732-73-8

Cover and text design by Katherine Robinson Coleman

Printed and bound in the United States of America.

Library of Congress Cataloging-in-Publication Data

Chilson, Richard.
  Meditation / by Richard Chilson.
      p. cm. — (Exploring a great spiritual practice)
  Includes bibliographical references.
  ISBN 1-893732-73-8 (pbk.)
  1. Meditation. I. Title. II. Series.
BL627 .C528 2004
204'.35—dc22
200302145

Contents

Introduction:	What Is Meditation?	9
Part One:	**Beginning a Practice**	**19**
chapter one	Making a Covenant	23
chapter two	Basic Types of Meditation	29
	The Body in Meditation	31
	Standing Meditation	35
	Sitting Meditation	38
	The Breath in Meditation	43
	Meditation With Words	47
	Meditation With the Mind	49
chapter three	Expanding Our Practice	55
	Misconceptions About Meditation	55
	Obstacles to Practice	60
	The Body and Its Complaints	68
chapter four	The Meditative Environment	75
	Moral Prerequisites	76
	The Community	83
	The Teacher	86
	Intellectual Environment	88
	Exoteric and Esoteric Teaching	90

Part Two: Meditation in the Spiritual Traditions   **93**

chapter five   Why Are Spiritual Traditions Important?   95

                  Beginnings of Meditation   99

chapter six   The Traditions of India   103

                  Yoga and Body Prayer   106

                  Buddhism   115

chapter seven Far Eastern Traditions   135

                  Tai Chi Chuan   137

                  Zen Buddhism   142

chapter eight   Western Spiritual Traditions   149

                  Judaism   149

                  Christianity   156

                  Islam   170

Part Three: The Royal Road of Spiritual Growth   **181**

chapter nine   The Ox Herding Pictures   183

    1.   Searching for the Ox   184

    2.   Discovering Footprints   185

    3.   Glimpsing the Ox   186

    4.   Seizing the Ox   188

    5.   Taming the Ox   189

    6.   Riding the Ox Home   191

    7.   Letting Go of the Ox   191

    8.   Ox and Self Both Forgotten   193

    9.   Returning to the Source   195

    10.   In Town With Open Hands   196

chapter ten   Meditation: Walking the Labyrinth   199
chapter eleven A Modern Map: Integral Psychology   205
                Archaic-Instinctual   207
                Magical-Animistic   210
                Power Gods   211
                Mythic Order   212
                Scientific Achievement   213
                The Sensitive Self   214
                Subtle and Causal Realms 218

Glossary   223

Introduction

What Is Meditation?

A man approached the **Buddha** curious about his teachings and his life. So he asked the Buddha, "Who are you? Are you a man?"

"No."

"Are you a god?"

"No."

"Then who are you?"

"I am awake," replied the Buddha.

Buddhist story

Meditation may appear a mysterious, mystical process or a fairly simple practice. It occurs in most spiritual and religious traditions and even in so-called "secular spiritualities."

But what is meditation? Can such an infinite variety of practices and theories be gathered under one name? Meditation is a discipline that enables a person to become more aware of the total field of experience.

We all filter our experiences. Although we are unaware of this process, it is a constant aspect of our life. In meditation we pull back from this automatic filtering and begin to allow more of the flow of experience to enter into awareness.

Meditation is the practice of simple awareness. This does not mean identifying what is happening or judging what is happening. To meditate is to simply be conscious of what is going on.

Buddhism calls it "stopping and seeing". First we learn to calm the mind, to stop the flow of thoughts. Then we begin to see what is actually happening. Christianity describes meditation as practicing the presence of God, or a practice that transforms us in Christ, or practice that unites us to God. We might see it as a method to discern the will of God. Meditation is a way to expand consciousness, a path to fuller awareness: enlightenment, a journey to the Real.

Some Definitions of Meditation

Meditation in its essence is the art of being aware, aware of what is going on inside you and around you.

OSHO

Meditation is not excitement, but concentration on our usual everyday routine.

Shunryu Suzuki

Thoughtful action to establish order. Meditation is nothing other than a relaxation technique with various larger purposes.

Andrew Weil

Meditation must be used as a tool to come to the freedom beyond tools.

Jack Kornfield

Is meditation like hypnosis? No, it's de-hypnosis.

Thai Meditation teacher

Why meditate? Meditation lowers blood pressure, lessens stress, helps us sleep, boosts energy, speeds recovery from illness, helps lessen asthmatic attacks, and helps with other allergic reactions. It reduces physical pain, helps overcome

Why meditate?

Meditation lowers blood pressure, lessens stress, helps us sleep, boosts energy, speeds recovery from illness. . .

addictions, improves response time, motor skills, and physical responses. Science shows evidence of all these effects.

Are there also harmful effects? Not really, as long as we follow directions. For example, it is good to meditate about 40 minutes a day. But if 40 minutes is good wouldn't 80 or 160 would be even better? No. Such concentrated meditation (which is done on meditation retreats) can release suppressed memories and energies which can be overwhelming. In a retreat the director can guide and help you, but on your own what will you do? The traditions will keep you safe. **Trust them.** Keep to them.

Meditation is not recommended for people suffering overwhelming anxiety or prone to psychosis. Otherwise normal neurotics can benefit from it and should be free from dangers. If you are under psychiatric treatment check with your doctor before beginning, just in case, but meditation is usually therapeutic.

Psychologically, meditation improves emotional stability, helps us find independence, helps us be more spontaneous, gives us better judgment, and improves our memory and intelligence.

But a spiritual seeker is more interested in the spiritual effects. Here we can say simply that meditation opens you more to what truly is. It is the art of being aware of what is inside you and what is outside you. It is a method of discovering and uniting you to who you and the world truly are. The Buddhist calls it nirvana; the Christian, the Kingdom of God. The Muslim and Jew simply God. Whatever the Real is, it is beyond all words or thoughts to accurately describe. We cannot understand it, but we can experience it. So we meditate.

One night the Baal Shem Tov was coming back from the river as was his custom. Each night he would go to the river since it was calm and quiet. What did he do there? He simply watched—the river, himself, the world.

But this night as he passed a rich man's house the watchman was standing at the door. The watchman had seen him going and coming night after night. So one night he asked, "Why do you go to the river night after night? I have followed you many times, yet you simply sit there for hours."

Baal Shem Tov said, "I know that you have followed me. The night is so quiet I can hear your footsteps. But I am curious about you too. What do you do?"

"I am a simple watchman," he said.

"But so am I," replied Baal Shem Tov.

"I don't understand. If you are a watchman you should be watching some house, some palace. What do you watch sitting there in the sand?"

"Ah, there is a difference," said Baal Shem Tov. "You are watching for somebody outside who may enter the house. I simply watch this watcher.

Who is this watcher? I watch myself."

"But that is ridiculous. Who would pay you?" said the watchman.

"Oh, but it is so wonderful that it pays for itself," replied Baal Shem Tov.

"This is strange. I have been watching my entire life. Yet I never had such a beautiful experience. Tomorrow night I will come with you. Teach me."

"I know how to watch — it seems only a different direction is necessary. You watch in some different direction. Teach me."

Jewish story

Let us begin with an experiment. I ask you with utmost sincerity to do this practice. Skipping it will do no good, and will keep you from the very experience you seek—meditation.

This meditation is called Sensing, Listening, and Seeing. It comes from a modern mystic master, Gurdjieff, who claimed to have encountered the hidden wisdom of the ages. In five to ten minutes it will provide a taste of the meditation experience—richer than a mere verbal description.

Read through the directions first, then do the exercise. It is not difficult. Don't complicate it. A major lesson meditation has to teach us is Keep it simple. Also, do not consider this just a preliminary to meditation. Do it with awareness. Make it a meditation in itself. Everything in our lives can become meditation. It is irrelevant whether it is doing dishes, driving, or just sitting. Awareness makes the difference.

Sensing, Listening, and Seeing

- *Sit down in a chair. Preferably a straight-backed, hard chair.*
- *Place both feet on the ground.*
- *Put your hands on your knees, palms down.*
- *Keep your back straight but not rigid.*
- *Close your eyes.*
- *Begin to scan your body.*

Start at the top of your head. Feel it. Sense it.

Now begin to descend through the body.

Parts may be quite sensitive.

Parts may be dull or even dead.

Simply be aware of whatever you sense. No need to name it. No need to judge. To analyze. To comment on.

Just sensing. Whatever is, is good. Whatever is not, is good.

Proceed from the top of your head

down through your neck

out into your arms

down the torso

down into the legs

and into the feet.

Simply sense your body.

If you find yourself wandering from the practice, when you notice this, simply return to the practice: no blame, no judgment.

Just begin sensing again.

Now, continuing to sense your body, pay attention to what you hear.

Listen! Do not try to identify the sounds. Pretend they are a symphony—a harmony of sounds. Do not label them pleasant or unpleasant; let every sound come to you, be received by you.

Continue a few minutes, sensing and listening.

Now, continuing to sense and listen, add seeing.

Open your eyes. See what is before you. No need to look around.

Gaze ahead softly.

Don't label, don't judge, don't identify with liking or disliking.

Just register what occurs. Spend a few minutes here.

You are sensing, listening and seeing. You are not thinking. Of course, thinking will occur. That's all right.

When you realize you are thinking, simply stop. No guilt. No grief. No regret.

Go back to sensing, listening, seeing.

After a time, slowly come out of the meditation.

Let go gradually. Try not to jump out of it. You may have gone deeper than you realized.

Congratulations! You've just meditated.

Take a moment; reflect on what happened. How do you feel now as compared to how you felt before? It may be very subtle. Take some time. Are you calmer? More focused? More at peace? More agitated? More confused? More relaxed? More in the present? Less of any of the above? Do not let this text put words to your experience. You are your best teacher.

Let the beauty you love be what you do. There are a thousand ways to kneel and kiss the earth.

Rumi

Here are some typical responses to meditation: Occasionally someone will say they felt nothing at all. Most people say they feel peaceful and relaxed. Many feel energized. Some feel a tingling and ecstasy. And a very few report an energy they feel they cannot control. If you feel more tired and stressed you were probably trying too hard. Relax. Be gentle with yourself. Go easy.

What is your experience? This is the most important and most difficult part. Do not discount it. Do not let another define your experience. Claim it. Own it. This is all you know. For you, this and only this is true.

This is meditation: a practice that over time can lead you to the truth. It does not act alone. It is aligned with various spiritual traditions. These traditions guide the meditator along the path of life. So the various paths, whether Christian, Jewish, Muslim, Buddhist, Taoist, Hindu, or other, explain and guide the meditative experience. There is no such thing as a truly objective meditative experience. Do the various paths lead to the same Ultimate? Who knows when that Ultimate is beyond all thought or words?

Beginning a Practice

Throughout this book you will encounter Ox Herding Pictures. Asian spiritualities have used them to show beginners the stages of meditation. They are not restricted to Zen and appear in other cultures as the Elephant pictures in Tibet and the Horse Training Pictures in Taoism.

A twelfth century Chinese Rinzai Zen master Kakuan Shion created the traditional set. The ox symbolizes our essential nature (Buddha nature), which we are seeking. The boy represents ourselves doing the seeking.

We will discuss these pictures later on in the book. For now, as you encounter each picture and text, see what it reveals about your own journey.

These pictures are not meant for the mind. It does no good to try to discover what they mean in an objective way. They speak to the heart as they enable us to begin to understand and appreciate our own experience. Without the practice of meditation the pictures are useless.

Finally, try not to look at the pictures as a series of stages—each succeeding stage somehow better than or superior to the previous ones. Look at the series as a circle rather than a ladder. Each stage is valuable and essential; no one better than another; each is simply part of the whole. We will not be complete when we have finished the journey. Rather, where we are now is good. Appreciate and open up to each step along the way. The step is the journey and the journey is all.

1. Searching for the Ox

In this world's pastures
I search, always looking for
the ox!
Mountain and stream I follow,
searching everywhere!
Exhausted, worn out, I don't
know where to turn.
I hear only the cicadas chirping in
the nighttime wood.

Comment: The ox is not really
lost; it is our true nature—
how can it be far from us? But
somehow I cannot see it.
Meditation may help.

exploring a great spiritual practice

chapterone

- - - - - - - - - - -

Making a
Covenant

We live in an age in which spiritual practices are easily available. That is the good news: To learn to meditate we do not need to rely upon an institution or teacher who will decide whether we are ready for this practice or not.

Some ancient traditions, including the Jewish and Christian, discouraged lay people from practicing meditation. Only a chosen few, who often devoted their lives to spiritual pursuit, were permitted. The rest of us were told to pray as best we could and go about our lives. That has changed today even within these institutions. Meditation classes and groups in churches and synagogues are as easily available as Eastern schools and teachers.

The downside of this easy convenience is that it is given outside of a controlled environment. A monk or nun is in an environment supportive of, and even conducive to, the practice. At special times each day the community gathers to meditate in common. Time is made available for private meditation as well. Monastic life exists ideally to support spiritual development.

But we are out in the world with jobs, families, commitments. How will we insert meditation into those busy lives? No structure supports us. We must find a way to enable our practice.

We must create a practice for ourselves. We cannot realistically model it upon the monastic pattern. We must find a way to fit it into our lives. Yes, we may have to make changes in our life. We may decide to rise a little earlier in the morning, or we may choose to give up a little television time. But no one can tell us what to do. We must be our own teachers here. One size certainly cannot fit all anymore. Even people in religious life today have to accommodate to a meditation practice.

How long should we practice daily? And daily practice is crucial. Once a week will not work. About twenty minutes, twice a day is the traditional advice—a good norm. To practice significantly more than an hour a day without a teacher's guidance or a community's support may open us too quickly to experiences beyond our ability to absorb. Less than twenty minutes a day is too little.

How should we start? If you are just starting out, forty minutes may be too much to swallow before you have sufficient experience to convince you that this is really beneficial. In meditation you will do battle with your greatest enemy—yourself, your ego. It will try to trip you up because it senses a threat to itself in all real spiritual work. It may begin by generating enthusiasm. This is great! Why not really commit to an hour a day! But what happens about a week later, when you are struggling with an hour a day? You are bound to give up. There's no time, no energy, no enthusiasm. And if you do persevere through sheer will power you are still going against the grain of the practice, which, as we will see, involves surrender.

We must be crafty. As Jesus said, we must be wise as serpents, gentle as doves. Only then may we tame the ego and truly bring it into the service of the Good. So begin slowly. How about ten minutes a day? Try that for one week. Then, if you feel good about it, add a couple more minutes.

When you reach twenty minutes a day, divide the meditation into two periods of ten minutes each. Continue to add a couple minutes a week. In twelve weeks you will be practicing twenty minutes twice a day. And even if it takes you twenty-four weeks that is infinitely better than biting off more than you can chew at the beginning and dropping out in a couple weeks or months. Hopefully, you will meditate for the rest of your life. Make haste slowly.

When are you going to meditate? Morning after rising and evening before retiring are the traditional times. But you may not be a morning person. Or the meditation may make you sleepy rather than wake you up. Or meditation in the evening may wake you up rather than calm you for sleep. You are your best teacher. Trust your experience. And remain open to how it might lead and change you.

Starting off, when can you find ten minutes a day? Take some time to think about it. Draw up a typical schedule for your day. When do you get up? Work? Play? Eat? Relax? Where can you insert ten minutes when you are calm and will not be disturbed? If you have children, when will you be safe from interruptions? When they are in bed? When is your spouse home, able and willing tend to them? Consider this now and locate time for a daily ten minute session.

When is it?

Make a contract.

I will meditate each day at _____.

Where will you meditate? A church or sacred space is ideal but rather far-fetched. Is there some quiet place easily available where you will not be disturbed? It may just be the corner of a room.

You might use a small table for an altar. Place a picture or an object that is sacred for you on it. Add a candle and maybe incense. Keep it simple. You actually do not need any more than a firm chair or, if you are flexible, a cushion.

Add this to your contract:

I will dedicate _____
as a space for my practice.

2. Discovering Footprints

Along the river I search,
under the trees—tracks!
Are those prints in the sweet
grass?
I find them even in the distant hills;
his nose to the heavens, none can hide him.

見跡

Comment: Soon I realize that
I must look into my own
mind. Perhaps a teacher woke
me up to see the footprints.
I am on my way.

exploring a great spiritual practice

chaptertwo

BasicTypesof
Meditation

There are really only a few primary types of meditation, each with an infinite number of variations. From a spiritual perspective, there are certain fundamental dimensions of being human that are focused at different points of our body. This notion of spiritual centers is highly developed in Eastern traditions, but it is found in the West as well. In making the sign of the cross, a Christian blesses and prays for the opening of these basic centers. The forehead points to the mind, the stomach to the body, and the crossing of the heart to the emotions. Indeed this blessing summarizes the entire Christian spiritual journey: to balance the mind and the body through the heart. The Jewish tradition recognizes these centers through the wearing of the phylacteries.

But spiritual centers figure most prominently in Eastern traditions—the seven chakras of Hindu and Buddhist systems, the acupressure points of Chinese medicine. Do not get bogged down in names and numbers. They are spiritual metaphors that point beyond the physical. Are there really seven, nine, or two hundred thirty? Irrelevant. We shall only consider the most important and only to help us explore the basic forms of meditation.

Buddhists define the human being as body, speech, and mind. We are a body: not in a body, certainly not trapped in a body. We are embodied beings. The body has sometimes been disparaged by spiritual people. Platonists and many Christians thought of humans as spirits imprisoned within a body. They did this by ignoring the very crucial Christian belief in the resurrection of the body: it will not be sloughed off in the new life but transformed and glorified.

In meditation, try to befriend the body no matter which tradition you take up. The body is your vehicle for experiencing the world. You are searching for wholeness and the body must partake in that wholeness.

The second aspect of the human being is the speech, which includes the breath. Breath is a vital component in most spiritual traditions. For Christians, Jesus is the Word that is God, and the primary symbol for the Holy Spirit is the breath.

Mind, the third spiritual dimension, includes but is not limited to intellect. In Buddhism mind is another term for heart. It is the inner aspect of the human being, body being the outer dimension and breath the bridge between. In Buddhism, mind is the most important dimension, while in Christianity the heart is. But since for Buddhism mind really is heart, the difference would appear semantic.

The Body in Meditation

The body is often ignored in the West. Indeed, some traditional Western postures are counterproductive. Kneeling is not good and entered Christianity as a result of courtly behavior. As vassals knelt before Lords, so the Christian should kneel before God. The original Christian posture for prayer is standing—a sign of the resurrection.

The body is an essential element of our being. It can help us enter into meditation and can even serve as the focus. St. Francis called his body "Brother Ass." That is apt. The body is dumb. The mind is subtle and apt to deceive. Trust the body. It will tell you what is true.

A number of different postures are common in meditation All have the same function: to make the body balanced, stable, and relaxed so that it conduces to, or at least does not interfere with, the practice.

Some traditions have a standard posture, which they insist upon. This has led to Americans sitting on the ground on meditation cushions (zafus) or benches. This is fine, provided your body is agile enough, but it is not necessary. A hard chair works just as well.

You are the only one to judge whether a posture is right for you. Take into consideration your physical history. Do you have arthritis or back problems? Do you tend to fall asleep easily? You want to adopt a posture that will keep you relaxed but alert and that you will be able to hold for about twenty minutes.

Do not regard this next set of instructions as merely preparation for meditation. Make it a meditation. Be mindful. Be aware. This is your experience. Honor it.

These forms are not the means of obtaining the right state of mind. To take this posture is itself to have the right state of mind. There is no need to obtain some special state of mind.

Soto Zen Teaching

Finding your center

This preliminary practice will help you get oriented toward your body and how you inhabit it.

First, stand up. Stand straight but not rigid.

Now look at your feet. Are they parallel to one another? This is deceptive. To be truly parallel they will seem a little closer to one another at the heels and a little farther apart at the toes.

If they are not parallel make them so now.

Now go back and forth between your original stance and the parallel stance.

Notice the difference throughout your body. It will be subtle but there is a difference. Sense it.

Allow the sensation to expand.

Exaggerate the positions of your feet if you need to. What is the difference? In which position do you feel most comfortable? Most balanced? Most relaxed?

Now focus on where you balance on your feet.

Is your center, your weight, over the arches, or is it over the heels or the toes?

Experiment with what it feels like to balance over each of these three positions.

Put your weight over your heels. Lean back just a little. You may feel your toes are about to leave the floor. What is it like to balance like this? You are literally a pushover. Your balance and stability is pretty precarious.

Now shift the center of gravity to your toes and the front of your feet. What does that feel like?

Lean just a little forward. Your heels may feel lighter, they may even feel as though they were about to leave the floor.

Is this position more stable than with the center over the heels? Shift back and forth.

Be as aware as possible what each position feels like.

Now place the center of balance right over your arches. How does that feel? Do you feel more stable? More present?

More grounded? More rooted?

> *Shift between the three positions. Get to know them. Where do you habitually balance? What might it be like to balance over the arches?*

Listen
to your
body.

> *Don't take anyone's word for it.*
>
> *Listen to your body.*
>
> *Now move your awareness up to your knees. Are they locked or loose? A lot of us lock our knees.*
>
> *To see whether you have your knees locked—after all, if you do this routinely you may not even notice it—flex your knees just a little.*
>
> *They should be bent forward just a little.*

It should not be obvious—just a little flex.

Feel the difference. If you normally flex your knees, lock them—push them back until they straighten no more.

Move between both positions.

Allow the feelings or sensations to expand.

Let your body teach you.

Now sense with your entire body. Where is your center? Where do you live within your body? If you are primarily an intellect you probably reside in the head. If you are dominated by emotions you may be centered in the heart. And if you are an athlete or someone who uses the body for delicate work—you are undoubtedly centered in the body which traditionally is located a little below the naval.

Take some time with this experiment.

Imagine placing your consciousness in the head, in the heart, in the naval.

Sense what each is like.

As you conclude, allow conscientiousness to expand throughout your body. Feel your feet and your hands. Be gentle with yourself. Come back slowly to the outer world. You may have gone deeper than you thought.

Ideally we should be at home in all three centers. And we should use whichever center is appropriate for the work we are doing. We all experience being in the wrong center. When we are lost in our minds and walking, we are likely to trip. And if you try to deal with emotions from the mind or the body the results will be inappropriate, if not downright disastrous.

Return to this practice over the next few weeks. Become familiar with the experience of being in each of the three centers. Ask yourself once in a while which center you are operating out of and whether that is appropriate for the work at hand.

Standing Meditation

The martial arts employ standing meditation. It is mor.e rigorous than sitting, but it builds strength and has the advantage of placing the entire body at attention. Sitting meditation tends to focus awareness in the torso. The legs only call attention to themselves when they fall asleep or experience pangs. If you have a real tendency to fall asleep easily, standing meditation may be best for you, at least in the beginning.

Practice. . . .

First get up.

Place both feet parallel to one another about shoulder-width apart. Knees should be unlocked, slightly flexed. You may place your arms at your sides.

Use your consciousness rather than your strength to allow the soles to touch the ground.

Imagine your weight sinking into the ground and connecting to the center of the earth.

Do not use any strain or tension.

Find a comfortable way to maintain the posture.

Hold your head as though it is suspended from a string from above. Keep your shoulders low and loose so that your neck and back can let go of tension.

Your chest should neither be pushed up nor hollowed out.

Your abdomen should be relaxed, neither pushed out nor overly contracted.

Let your arms hang loose with your elbows relaxed and the palms facing downwards.

Breathe naturally through the nose. The mouth is closed lightly as are the teeth.

Your tongue rests upon the upper palate just behind your upper teeth.

Allow your gaze to be soft; focus on something about six feet in front of you on the ground.

Some martial arts ask you to put your arms out in front of you about the level of your upper chest. Bring the hands together, the right palm touching the back of the left hand, the thumbs touching. Your arms are not making a circle but an embrace. Obviously this posture will take working up to if you are not in good physical condition, but the position itself promotes physical fitness. And it places you at gentle attention, allows spiritual energy free circulation throughout the body, grounds your feet in the earth and your upper torso in the sky.

Most meditators do not stand, but if you are seeking physical health this is the most beneficial.

Sitting Meditation

■ ■ ■ ■ ■ ■ ■ ■ ■ ■ ■ ■ ■ ■ ■

The traditional Eastern lotus asana provides a solid balanced foundation. The legs, thighs, as well as buttocks are on the ground creating real stability. The Western cobbler posture—sitting with legs crossed—on the other hand is quite unstable. Try it and notice that the only points touching the ground are your buttocks and the sides of your feet. This is not a good posture for meditation. Now, if you can, try the half lotus, which is much easier than the full lotus:

Sit on a cushion with your buttocks toward the front so that your thighs and feet do not rest on the cushion but on the floor.

Now bend the left leg at the knee drawing the left foot into your crotch area. The foot should rest along with most of the leg and thigh on the floor.

Now take the right leg and rest it on top of the left.

Bend the right knee and place the right foot just over the left foot in your groin area.

The right thigh, leg, and foot should be resting upon the left.

Notice how stable the posture is.

Your buttocks, your thighs, legs and feet are making contact with the floor.

You are forming a solid tripod of stability.

This is the entire raison d'être for a sitting posture. If you are flexible you should consider making this your own meditation posture. Of course if you are limber enough to make and hold the full lotus you have the perfect posture. We will not describe the full lotus since it does demand full flexibility and would be beyond most readers' ability or desire. It can easily be found in any yoga book or class.

Unless you can do the Lotus posture or the half Lotus comfortably, it is best to sit in a chair. Choose a straight backed hard chair. A soft chair feels more comfortable but again it can lead to sleep. Preferably use a chair with no arms since they may interfere with the position of your own arms. Sit in the chair and place both feet on the ground. Notice how you feel. This itself is meditation—be aware!

Sit in the chair out from the back so that you, not the chair, are supporting your back.

With the buttocks and hips on the chair and both feet on the ground you should feel fairly stable and balanced. Feel it. This too is part of the meditation practice.

For obvious reasons sitting with legs crossed is discouraged. Try it; feel the difference.

What to do with your hands? The most obvious choice will be some position that will allow them to be relaxed. When they wander during meditation (and they probably will), once you notice their movement you can return them to the posture.

But there is more to the hand posture than simple relaxation. Our hands are very expressive. Some cultures have elaborately developed hand gestures.

In Sanskrit a hand posture is called a mudra and various mudras carry different meanings. In many pictures of the Buddha he is gently touching the earth with one hand. This refers to the fact that when the Buddha achieved enlightenment the earth shook in response. A Christian might place one hand over the other at a ninety-degree angle, with the palms up when receiving Holy Communion. This represents the cross, source of salvation or wholeness. The open palms facing upward witness an openness to God's gifts and graces. Try the gesture and feel the experience. So for your own posture you may want to take a mudra that symbolizes some aspect of your own spirituality.

It will be very subtle. You may even feel foolish, but you are becoming more sensitive to your body and that is part of the spiritual journey. Whatever you choose to do with your hands, place them so that they are relaxed, comfortable, and when you catch them wandering you'll know where they belong.

Now let us move on to the back. You want the back straight and relaxed, not rigid. Should you use the back of the chair? Again most traditions discourage this. Why? Primarily to keep you awake. I had a friend in seminary who was asleep five minutes after meditation began each day. If he had sat a little away from the back of the seat, supporting his own back, when he drifted off to sleep he would have swerved or hit the chair and awakened.

Spiritual energy runs up and down the spine, according to some traditions (Taoist, Buddhist, Yogic). To push the back into the chair can interfere with or block this energy. So although you must decide, know that most traditions encourage you to support your own spine. It is a vital part of the practice. Of course if you have any back problems or you experience pain, modify your posture accordingly. The basic requirement is a posture that keeps us alert but relaxed.

Meditation chairs, stools, and kneelers are available from supply stores. But you really don't need anything more than a good chair or a hard cushion if you sit on the ground. Anything else is icing on the cake, and may just be a distraction to keep you from starting to practice.

Practice. . . .

Keep the **neck** straight.
> Tuck in your chin just a little.
> This helps to straighten the neck.

Remember, midway between tension and relaxation.
> Find that place for yourself.

Now consider the **head.**

Relax your **jaw.**
> You might even massage it if it is tense or tight.
> Or practice yawning. Take a few really deep yawns.
> This is a wonderful way to relax the tension
> in both your jaw and your neck.

Allow your **lips** to open slightly.
> Place the tip of your **tongue** on your upper palette,
> the ridge of solid tissue just back of your upper front
> teeth.

Your **eyes** may be open or shut.
> If the environment is busy you will probably want to shut
> them.
> If you keep them open
>> gaze about six feet ahead of you on the floor.
>> Imagine a mother gazing lovingly at her child.
> The gaze is soft and gentle, not a stare.

Now you are ready to begin a meditation practice, whatever it may be. But every so often during the meditation, scan your body. Tension has a habit of creeping in again. When you notice tension, imagine it leaving your body when you exhale. That is enough. Be gentle. Have compassion on yourself.

The Breath in Meditation

The breath is an almost universal object for meditation. Christianity sees breath as the presence of the Holy Spirit within us. In Judaism the word for breath is *Ruach*, the spirit of God. In Sanskrit breath is *prana*, the intuitive wisdom that goes beyond words and concepts. In Chinese it is called *chi*.

These meditations will lead you into a deeper experience and appreciation of this simple activity. When you focus upon the breath, do not attempt to change it in any way. You will probably find it becomes more and more subtle. It will quiet. Then again at times it may deepen and even become agitated. Simply observe it. It will change on its own.

Counting the breath

A number of traditions use counting the breath to help the disciple calm the mind. Before you begin, tell yourself that you are going to do this practice as perfectly as possible. After all, meditation is work. But as you enter the practice relax.

Drop what tension you can. You have made a commitment, now simply do the practice. You might ask Allah, or God, or Mother Nature, to help you do this meditation. This can be an act of surrender for you—meditation will happen through the gift of grace, not through your own will power.

Take your meditation posture.

Now count each breath on the intake.

> *Count from one to ten, then begin again with one.*

> *If you lose count, simply begin again with one.*

> *Do not be frustrated if you cannot seem to make it to ten.*

>> *That is why you are practicing.*

>> *Failure to meet the goal can be a spur to further practice.*

> *At the end gently let go of the practice. Take some time to return to the outer world. When you are ready, open your eyes and maybe take a deep breath and stretch a little. Do not jump out of the practice. You do not know how deep you may have gone. Be gentle with yourself.*

Focusing on the breath in the nostrils

This time we will meditate on the breath again, but we will change the object of awareness. Remember how to enter into the practice; begin with the body and taking your posture. Be aware—this is not the prelude but part of the meditation. Spend the time you have set aside for meditation for this session. And come out of the practice gently.

Practice. . . .

As you meditate be aware of the breath
where it enters your nostrils.
Notice it. Be curious about it.
How does it feel? Is it warm or cold? Gentle or strong?

And as it leaves your body is it warm or cold?
Where do you actually feel the breath entering your nostrils?
Where do you actually feel it leaving your nostrils?
How is the entering and leaving different?

Awareness of the breath

Now we will focus on the full range of the breath. Practice this for at least one session.

Practice . . .

First, take your meditation posture.

Take a couple slow, deep breaths;
let the tension flow out as you exhale.

Turn your awareness to your breath

as it enters and leaves your body. Simply notice it.
Notice each breath. Its length. Its depth. Its feeling.
Pay attention to the entire breath.

Be aware of the pause

between the breathing in and breathing out as well.

What is the quality of the breath? How long to does it take? How does it feel?

Do not worry about labeling or what words to use.

Try to move beyond words. Contact the direct experience.

How does the breath change in the course of the session?

Where does it manifest in the body?

At what points does it manifest in what place?

Be curious.

See each breath as totally unique, never before experienced.

Cherish it, then let go and welcome the next.

There is no other like it. Experience each breath as fully as possible.

Come out gradually as you end.

Take a moment to savor the peace and relaxation.

In another meditation try to focus upon just that moment between breathing out and breathing in. Some teachers claim that at that moment you have the experience of enlightenment. Examine the moment—the stasis—the pause between in and out. What is it like? How does it begin? How does it end? It seems such a short space, but it is filled with infinite possibilities

Meditation With Words

E veryone who meditates is going to have to deal with thoughts. Fortunately there are techniques that aid us in controlling thoughts. Most spiritualities have used mantras—words and phrases—to focus the mind and help the practicioner to enter more profoundly into the meditative experience.

Mantras may be in the vernacular or a foreign language. Some traditions claim the sound of the words themselves has the power to penetrate reality. When we survey the spiritual traditions we will delve further into specific mantras. Here it is only necessary to choose a mantra for practice. For now, choose a mantra to use from the list below.

Common Mantras

OM, the primordial sound (Hindu)

OM MANI PADMA HUM, no real translation exists (Buddhist)

Hallelujah! Praise be to God (Jewish)

Jesus (Christian)

There is no God but Allah, and Mohammed is his messenger.

La ilaha ill-llah, Muhammad-un Rasulu-llah (Muslim)

One (Relaxation response, Secular Spirituality)

mantra

means

'word'

in Sanskrit

Practice . . .

Once you have chosen your mantra
take some time to settle into the meditation posture.

When you are ready, take up the mantra.
Say it over and over, many times.
You might even chant it.

After a while, allow the mantra to become silent, but
continue repeating it.
It now resides within you—in your mind, in your heart.

When you find yourself drifting away from the mantra
simply return to the practice.
No blame. No judgment. This is part of the practice.

Meditation With the Mind

Visualization focuses upon the mind and especially the faculty of imagination. This is a particularly important faculty for us to develop in our culture since we have generally banished the art of imagination from our lives. The act of reading asks us to enter into the story by visualizing the characters, the setting, the different events of the story. Radio demands more imagination than television. We are not as adept at visualization as our ancestors were simply because we are not encouraged to develop it. But it is a great help in our spiritual growth.

Imagination is the key faculty in the development of hope. We become hopeless when we cannot imagine another way of being or a way out of our present unsatisfactory state. Take away a person's ability to imagine and you take away a great deal of his or her freedom. Fortunately we all have this faculty, whether we have cultivated it or not. And meditation provides a wonderful means of developing it.

For the next meditation we shall imagine an idyllic, relaxing place. We are blessed with various kinds of imagination. We are not limited to the visual. In fact, some of us are not really gifted with visual imagination. Some are more attuned to sounds, or feelings, or sensations. Explore your own imagination. Use all of your senses to recreate this peaceful scene.

Practice. . . .

To begin, take up your meditation posture. And take it up slowly. Be aware of entering into it. It won't take more than a few seconds, but throughout your practice you want to guard against routine. Routine leads to numbness, not awareness. You are taking this posture here and now. You may have taken it before. You may have taken it thousands of times. But this is here. This is now. Be here now.

Take a couple of long deep breaths.

Relax.

For a few moments simply focus upon your breathing.

Allow the breath to bring you to your center.

If there is anything on your mind - things that need attending to -

tell yourself you will do them after the meditation.

Of course it is important that you be true to yourself.

What good will lying do?

If you can't deal with your distractions after this session,

find a time when you can and will.

Now, imagine one of your favorite places.

Choose a place associated with pleasant, happy experiences.

A place that is peaceful and relaxing.

> *The beach. Or the mountains. Or a favorite bench in a park. Find a place filled with good feelings for you.*

Allow the scene to refresh you.

Keep it light and playful. Relax into it. Don't try too hard.

Daydream a little, but keep the daydream focused on the scene.

Spend the rest of the session in this place.

When your mind wanders from the scene

> *gently return it to the practice.*

When you are done come back to the outer world gently and slowly.

> *How you leave off a meditation is as important*
>
> *as how you enter into one. All is part of the practice.*

Maybe you feel deficient in imagination. You are thinking you can't do this. Yes, you can. It is an innate human ability. We all have it. All it needs is practice. If you can't imagine the scene, pretend you are imagining it. That is enough. And if you can't even pretend, play that you are pretending.

3. Glimpsing the Ox

On a branch sings the nightingale;

warm sun, mild wind, a bank of willow.

The ox sleeps without a care, in full view, unhidden.

Who could draw that great head, those majestic horns!

見牛

Comment: I have found the path! What a relief!

But the ox is only seen, not grasped.

exploring a great spiritual practice

chapterthree

ExpandingOur Practice

Misconceptions About Meditation

Don't begin this chapter until you have been practicing meditation for at least one week. If you are having trouble practicing, ask yourself if you have bitten off too much. Is ten minutes too much to take out of your day? Really? If it isn't, then what is keeping you from meditating? Do you really want to meditate? Are you afraid of what meditation might demand of you? Are you afraid of where it might lead you?

Perhaps you have some idea of meditation that prevents you from practicing. Let us examine some common misperceptions about meditation. One of them may be preventing you from giving yourself over to the practice. And even if you are practicing, it is useful to examine what meditation is not so that we may more clearly understand what it is.

Meditation is not reserved for just a certain kind of person. We all have the capacity to meditate. Just because you find yourself distracted does not mean you are not meditating. That is part—in fact, a crucial part—of the practice. Meditation is not something reserved for monks and nuns and for people who do not engage in the world. Indeed, people who must interact with the world may need it more than those secluded in a safe environment.

Maybe you meditated and you feel that nothing happened. You may feel that you are missing something, that it is too difficult, or that you can't "get it." No. It is not difficult. It is quite easy to do but difficult to master. That is why it asks for a lifetime of practice. Everybody can do it. But can everyone commit to it over the long haul?

Perhaps you found it too easy. Perhaps you're thinking, "This can't help me," or "I can do this whenever I want." Well, try a little more. It will become more of a task, guaranteed.

People may tell you that meditation is the work of the devil; that you are opening yourself to evil powers. Fundamentalists are skeptical and afraid of meditation. Any religion that seeks to fully control its members is going to be afraid of any one member's personal experience of the All. The Christian Church in the past has been suspicious of mystics. Today fundamentalist Christians have such a fear of the devil that they might be said to have too little faith in the power of God. After all, if there is a God, who is really in charge? If God can be undermined so easily by evil, is that really God? Trust in the power of good. Trust in God. Trust in your own experience. How does meditation influence your life?

Are you afraid that if you meditate you will be brainwashed into some religion? While most religions support the practice of meditation, the practice itself is not wedded to any one religious tradition. Certainly the religious tradition colors and shapes the path the meditator walks but the practice itself is neutral.

Are you afraid that if you take up meditation you will be asked to do things or give up things you do not wish to do or give up? Will I have to sell all I have and go about begging? Will I have to become a monk or nun? Yes, when you meditate you are opening yourself to Absolute Reality, however you may choose to imagine it. Yes, you are on a path. But that path only asks you to take the next step that opens before you. And you have the freedom to take that step or to refuse it.

A spiritual truism says that God never gives you more than you can handle. On the other hand, St. Teresa of Avila once told God, "If this is the way you treat your friends, no wonder you have so few." No question: the spiritual journey is dangerous. But isn't this what you hunger for? Isn't this why you are interested to begin with? As Jesus taught, "Don't worry about tomorrow. Tomorrow will have troubles enough of its own. Just concentrate upon today." Why not take up the practice? It is gentle. It moves slowly.

Perhaps you're thinking, "What if I really like this meditation? Will I have to leave the world?" No. In fact meditation should help you to engage the world. It should make you more present to what is happening. It does not entrance you. It de-trances. It makes us able to see through our programming to what is really happening. Rather than an escape from reality, meditation helps us to engage with the real rather than with our illusions of what is real.

We may think that in order to meditate properly we need an ideal environment. We need to be like the monk or nun living in a monastery. If we think this then we have probably never experienced a monastic environment. Rather than protecting us from the world, a monastery makes the environment into a pressure cooker. In the world we can pretty much distance ourselves from people we do not like, people who drive us crazy. In a monastery that person is going to be sitting next to you for every meal for the rest of your life. There is no such thing as the perfect meditation environment. You cannot shut out the world. Why try?

Maybe you are expecting meditation to take you out of yourself. You may wish that it would produce an altered state of consciousness. Or perhaps you are afraid that is just what it will do. It will be weird. Relax. Meditation puts us more in touch with reality. It is not meant to take us out of the world or produce strange experiences.

This may be the most deadly pitfall for Americans. Some of us come to meditation after experiences induced by psychedelic drugs. We are looking for experiences. We are looking to "see God." Meditation is not about spiritual highs. It is about life. Down-to-earth life. It is simply about being here now. That is not a high, not an escape. That is reality.

Perhaps you are worried that you are not doing it right. You need a teacher. You need someone who can really confirm that you are doing it right. Well, in that case find a teacher. But you will be disappointed.

Any authentic teacher will tell you the same thing. Meditation is not some arcane, secret practice, at least in the beginning. It is a fairly simple activity. It is not difficult. But perfecting it is not at all easy. What it does demand is persistence. It demands practice. Day after day.

Once a novice was on an intensive retreat. On the third day as he gazed at the white wall in front of him, he began to see wonderful creatures. He saw dragons, angels, beautiful colors. He could not wait to tell the master. And when he finally had his session with the master and told him what was happening, his master said to him, "That's all right. Keep meditating. Soon all those things will disappear."

Zen story

Obstacles to Practice

There are really only two obstacles to meditation—dullness and agitation. The easiest prevention is to meditate when you are not too aroused or tired. Do not meditate for at least an hour after a heavy meal.

> *Disease, dullness, doubt, carelessness,*
> *laziness, worldly-mindedness, illusion,*
> *missing the point, instability—*
> *these are obstacles in Yoga.*
>
> *Patanjali*

We may be plagued by doubt, especially as Americans. Meditation is a conscious and free choice for us. We have usually had to search simply to find out that it exists. Many friends would regard meditation as useless or even dangerous. How do you know you have chosen wisely? Is this really the right thing for you?

But you are just beginning your practice. You have made no decision other than to give meditation a chance. So when such thoughts come up, acknowledge them and let them go. Make them part of your meditation.

Right now it is enough to acquaint ourselves with the various forms of meditation. But there will come a time when we will need to make a decision to adopt a kind of meditation and a tradition. Otherwise we remain spiritual butterflies, never lighting anywhere long enough to be changed. And transformation is why we approach meditation to begin with. At that point when we have to choose, doubt will again enter the picture. Is this the right practice, the right tradition, the right teacher? But that time is not now, so if doubt arises, acknowledge it and let it be.

Sit someplace free of distraction.

Focus on any doubts or worries you might have about meditation.

Be completely open to them,
do not censor any out.
Examine each carefully—
is it absurd?
is it valid?
Most will be instantly unmasked as absurd.

Consciously let go of each, one by one—
imagine it as a balloon that sails away. . .
and then vanishes out of sight.

A Meditation for Doubt *by Baba Ram Dass*

A deeper form of doubt may assail you—"am I doing this right?" Now, there is certainly a right and a wrong way to go about meditation. And some practices are extremely detailed and precise. But, especially for the beginner, the important thing is not whether you are doing it precisely but whether you are entering into the spirit of meditation. That spirit is the constant practice of awareness. So ask yourself: Am I doing this with the right attitude, including being open to being taught? Am I being gentle and patient? Am I present to the moment?

A spiritual teacher was rowing a boat along a lake shore.
He heard someone chanting the word, "Alleluia".

> *Ah, thought the teacher, they are chanting the most powerful prayer.*

They say that if you chant it properly
all kinds of powers will be given to you.
Now I have never experienced those powers,
but I do know that the teachers all say you must chant the word
as Al-LE-lu-ia
and this poor student is chanting Al-le-LU-ia.
I should help him.

> *So the teacher beached his boat*

and entered the student's hut.
He told the student that the practice of the chant
granted wonderful powers.
But he had also heard that the chant
was properly sung as Al-LE-lu-ia.
The student was very grateful for this teaching.

And as the teacher left and returned to his boat
he heard the student chanting, Al-LE-lu-ia.

The teacher felt very good that he had helped this
student.

But as he drifted out into the lake again he
heard the chant change.

Now the student was back to his
old ways, chanting Al-le-LU-ia.

Ah, the depths of human
sinfulness and ignorance, sighed
the teacher.

A few minutes later a touch to
his shoulder startled him.

He looked around and saw the
student walking on the water.

"I'm sorry, great teacher, but could you
teach me the correct chant again?"

Sufi story

It won't be long in your practice before you realize you are bored. Maybe this has already happened. Welcome to the real world of practice. Boredom is one of the greatest obstacles and there is no magic way to vanquish it. When boredom occurs, pay attention: how does it feel? Where does it reside in your body? What thoughts are associated with it? Make boredom your object of meditation.

You will find that although it tries to convince you this is the way things are, if you persevere you will discover boredom too is impermanent. It is not a reality. It is merely a state of mind like anger, joy, fear. Confronting it and getting to know it is part of the practice.

A monk approached the teacher and complained.
He did not want to continue:
it was so boring observing each breath.
The master grabbed him by the hair,
shoved his head under a bowl of water nearby,
and held him under for a couple minutes.
When he released the monk, he asked,
"How bored are you now in observing the breath?"

Zen story

Drowsiness is not the same as boredom. You try to meditate and you feel sleepy, or you actually fall asleep. First, are you getting enough sleep? Many of us do not; between seven and eight hours of sleep a night is recommended. Listen to your body—that is your meditation lesson right now.

You may also experience drowsiness because you are touching feelings you do not want to experience. On one meditation intensive there came times when I just could not keep my eyes open, I felt cold, and I literally went numb mentally. I was not ready to receive what the practice gave me at that time. My psyche was protecting itself. Here a teacher and a community can be invaluable. Sluggishness can be a sign of pain or sorrow we don't want to feel. Examine it for the root cause. Work through it with your focused mind.

Drowsiness can occur even though we are well rested and are not confronting something we wish to avoid. When that happens, change your posture. Try standing up to meditate. Or try the bellows breath (right) to give yourself a second wind.

Sloth, not the same as drowsiness but another key hindrance, means neglecting what is essential and wasting time on inessentials. If you believe meditation is really important then you need to practice whether you want to or not. Lots of times it will seem an almost impossible task to sit down to meditate. This is sloth. There is a reason that monks regard it as the most deadly of the seven sins; for their life of prayer and meditation, it is.

Bellows Breath

This is not a meditation but an aid to meditation. You can use this breath whenever you need it throughout the day or during practice.

∽ Sitting in your posture, close your mouth and
place the tongue on the upper palate.

∽ Now using your belly as a bellows
inhale and exhale quickly for at least 15 seconds.

∽ You will hear the air as it rushes into and out of your nostrils: short quick breaths.

∽ When you are finished, resume normal breathing.

∽ How do you feel?

∽ You'll probably feel refreshed and invigorated.

A Journalist once asked Dr. Martin Luther King, Jr., how he **found the time** to do all the things he accomplished in the course of a day. "When I get up in the morning, " replied Dr. King, "I give the **first hour** to **God.** And **God gives me** the **rest.**"

Dr. Martin Luther King, Jr.

Living in the world we may be more tempted by greed, anger, or lust, but as far as our spiritual practice is concerned sloth is the demon. Monasteries have common disciplines. The entire community comes together to meditate at certain times. But we have to create our own times for meditation. Then we must find ways to remain faithful to our schedule.

Overcoming sloth is part of the practice, just as is overcoming boredom and the other distractions. Examine sloth. What does it feel like? Can you discover what triggers it? Watch it and see that it too is not constant; it comes and goes. But persevere with practice. And when you do give up, as quickly as possible return to the practice. Don't get down on yourself. Don't do a guilt trip. Just return to meditation.

Under the general heading of "agitation" we might be too

excited to meditate. We have other things to do. We don't have time. If you find it impossible to sit, do walking meditation. Take some slow deep breaths—that often helps to slow down. Join a community of meditators who can encourage and offer support when things get rough. Above all, don't give up. What you are doing will help with all of these obstacles eventually. You are on the right path.

Finally, with all these hindrances, do not fight them. Opposition gives them tremendous power. Allow them to move through you. Examine them with awareness and nonresistance. This softens them. They can be great teachers. Listen to them.

If obstacles occur during the meditation itself name them. "Boredom." "Tired." "Fear." Naming them a couple of times often dissolves them. As you practice you also develop the virtues of patience, calm, and balance, which will aid you on your journey.

It is normal for your mind to want to wander, to draw your attention to issues that are blocks for you, to entertain itself, and to plan for the future. You are still meditating while this is going on. The hindrances are a sign that your meditation is working, not that you cannot do this. If you experience no hindrances and distractions or obstacles, then chances are you are trying too hard. Let go. Relax. Be gentle with yourself. Have compassion.

The Body and Its Complaints

No matter which posture we assume, when we are immobile over time aches and pains are bound to arise. Or we may be distracted by outside noises or by flies. What are we to do? First, we may want to look at our attitude toward these "obstructions." What happens if we cease trying to fight them and simply accept their presence?

Do not try to drive pain away by pretending
that it is not real.
Pain, if you seek serenity in Oneness,
will vanish of its own accord.

Sengstan

I once attended a year-long meditation class that met twice a week. As I walked up to the building one day, I could not escape the fact that workers were digging up the street right in front of the building and that a jackhammer was an essential part of this effort. My stomach sank. How can we possibly have a decent class with this racket going on just outside? Since I had already walked for twenty minutes to get to class, I figured I might as well give it a try. Thankfully, the teacher was sensitive to the possibility of this being perceived as an obstacle. But rather than tell us that it would be impossible to meditate this day he suggested that we use the jackhammer as the focus of our meditation. Instead of the useless attempt to shut it out, to invite it into our consciousness. What did it sound like? To try to hear it as simply sound. Not good. Not bad. Just sound. Although the meditation was still difficult, it was possible.

Something need only be a distraction if we label it so. Befriend the distractions—they may have something valuable to teach. Take whatever you are given. You cannot change it. Accept it. Give up judgments. Give up expectations. And practice. That is all that is asked—practice.

One day a student approached his teacher during a meditation intensive. He was quite happy. "Teacher, for the first time today I was able to sit without my legs falling asleep."

"That is terrible, my son," replied the teacher. "What will keep you awake now?"

Zen story

We have looked at a proper meditation posture. Now we can refine it. As you develop your practice and can take the posture instinctively, before beginning meditation proper it is a good idea to scan your body. First, this puts you in contact with your body. Second, it is an easy way to enter into a state of awareness: a good technique for passing over from ordinary consciousness into meditative awareness.

Practice. . .

Scanning the body

Take your meditation posture.
Take a couple of deep relaxing breaths.

Now, begin to place your awareness in different parts of your body.

Begin with the crown of your head.

Slowly allow your focused awareness to sink down
to the area of your eyes and ears,
then to your cheeks,
down to the jaw,

and continue slowly moving down your body.
Shoulders, down the arms to hands to the tips of your fingers,
down the chest, to the stomach,
hips, thighs, feet, toes.

Take your time. Get to know your body.
Appreciate it. Savor it.

There may be areas you cannot feel.
That is all right. Simply note that.

Other places may be tense or even painful.
  Again simply notice.

As with all practice, keep it fresh. All practices tend to become routine and in doing so lose their value.

How your body feels today and now is different from how it felt yesterday or even an hour ago.

Practice being in the present.

Awareness of your body is an effective way to bring yourself into the present.

By this point you may believe you have to be still to meditate. Not at all. Walking is a wonderful meditation. In communities that practice a lot of meditation, sitting meditation alternates with walking meditation. In this way the body does not become stressed and rebellious. On a Zen *seshin* you sit for twenty-five minutes, then walk for ten, then sit again for twenty-five minutes. On such a schedule of sitting and walking you can meditate for significant amounts of time. If sitting still drives you crazy at first consider using walking meditation as your primary practice. Only you can discover which is the right path for you.

Practice. . . .

Walking Meditation

Stand upright.
  Join your hands together behind your back
    or allow them to fall to your sides.

Now take small slow steps.

Be aware of each movement.

Do not go so slowly that you lose your balance,
  but go slowly enough so that you can be aware
  of each phase of the step.

Depending on the space where you practice
  you may choose to walk in a circle
  or back and forth in a line.

Allow the experience of walking to expand for you.

There is an infinite world of experience and awareness
  to be found in this simple physical action.

4. Seizing the Ox

With all my might I seize
him.

But he is wild; awesome
in power.

He charges the high plateau,
   mountain clouds hide him.

On an impenetrable mountain-pass
he stands.

Comment: I have begun to
see my mind. And now I
experience just how wild it is.
If I wish the ox to submit, I
must use discipline.

exploring a great spiritual practice

chapterfour

The Meditative Environment

We have already discussed creating a physical environment conducive to meditation and we have considered the ideal length and times for meditation when we created our meditation covenant. Now let us look at some other aspects of the meditation environment which will aid us in developing a stable practice.

As you increase your practice time, look for times ideal for your practice. Try not to meditate just after a big meal, but better to do it then than never. Are you more awake in the morning? Then you might want to get up just twenty minutes earlier to meditate. How about at night just before bed? Perhaps you are too tired then, or, you might find meditation a wonderful sedative. Maybe you have a little time when you get home from work before dinner. Where can you take little meditation breaks during the day? It doesn't have to be a long time. Take a break while waiting for the children to get out of school. Take a break if you arrive a few minutes early for a movie. Take a break waiting in your car for a train to pass by. These little breaks help the practice seep into our ordinary lives and bring us a little more awareness.

You may also want to take some quality time to devote to meditation. Retreats are very popular today at numerous centers throughout the country. They often fill up early so plan in advance. On a retreat you might spend up to ten hours a day in sitting and walking meditation. There will also be lectures and opportunities to meet with the retreat leader to ask questions and discuss your experience and practice. These intensives offer a real boost to practice and many people schedule at least one week yearly.

Since most of us do not live in a meditative community we must be creative in devising our schedules for practice. We must consider our lives and ourselves. What works? What doesn't? This growing awareness of who we are as meditators is itself a meditation.

Moral Prerequisites

The meditative traditions are unanimous in demandin.g a life that conduces to spiritual development and growth as a foundation for practice. At the minimum this means that those who practice meditation are leading a moral life.

There are many definitions of the moral life and there is some disagreement between the emphases in the different traditions. But there is no doubt concerning the basics, whether the Judeo-Christian Ten Commandments, the Principles of Islam, or the Precepts of Buddhism. Do good and avoid evil. And doing good means at the very least not harming ourselves or others.

I am the Lord your God.
Do not make what is not God into a god.
Do not take your connection to God lightly or easily.
Spend one day a week in prayer and play.
Honor your father and mother.
Do not kill.
Do not commit adultery.
Do not steal
Do not lie.
Do not crave what is not yours.

The Ten Commandments

Because Buddhism is geared specifically toward a life of meditation and because many, especially those who are not Christian or Jewish, find it simpler and more fundamental than the Ten Commandments, we shall use it to explore what a moral foundation for meditation involves. These precepts are quite practical and down to earth. They are meant to guide us toward a lifestyle in which we no longer harm ourselves or others.

The first precept tells us to refrain from killing. Now most of us do not think of ourselves as killers. But are we hunters? Do we kill wild animals? Are we soldiers? Do we enjoy computer games based upon killing? Do we subject ourselves continually to violent entertainment? What impact does this have upon our consciousness?

Some people may take this precept to the point where they becomes vegetarians. Others who cannot or do not want to become vegetarians may distance themselves from the killing of animals by having others do it for them. In Tibet the butchers were Muslims; once the animal was killed the Buddhists felt they could eat it. After all it is very difficult to survive in Tibet as a vegetarian. How we understand this precept in our own circumstances will vary and it will also change as we progress along the spiritual path.

The second precept concerns stealing, which extends to not cheating on one's taxes, and to taking only one's fair share of the world's resources. Are we conscious of what we take for

No man is an island.

John Donne

ourselves? Do we have more than we need so that someone else suffers hardship?

Meditation will reveal our interconnectedness. As the great Christian preacher John Donne claimed, "No man is an island." Even before we have attained this experience we can begin to put it into practice. This practice will actually help us achieve the insight. How do we share the earth with one another? This includes not only other human beings but the other creatures of our planet. Does our consumption harm their own lives and environments? How can we tread the earth more lightly?

The third precept turns our attention to our speech. One branch of the Eightfold Path is Right Speech. We may be surprised that speech should be a major moral foundation. After all, it is just words. Yet how powerful words are! They reveal who we are, what we are feeling, what we are thinking. They can heal and hurt. They can lead to war or peace.

Yet how **powerful words are!** ... They can **heal** and **hurt.** They can **lead** to **war** or **peace.**

Once a **healer** came to visit a sick person. He spoke a few words in prayer with the patient. And as he turned to go a skeptic in the crowd murmured that this was a rather **superficial way of healing**. The healer turned to him and said, "You do not know what you are saying. You are an ignorant fool!" The skeptic took great offense at such a response; he shook with anger and his face turned bright red. The healer said, **"If just a few words** are able to make you **so angry** why should not **other words** have the **power to heal?"**

Sufi healing story

Take a look at your words. Are you a person of few words? Or do you like to talk a lot? And what is the content of that speech? Is it idle? Gossip? Hurtful of others? Addicted to vulgarity or profanity? Are you given to grandiosity, or on the other hand, false humility? Are you aware of your speech, or do you find your mouth often running ahead of your mind so that you blurt out hurtful or stupid words? Do you use speech as a defense? Do you avoid serious speech by slipping into humor? Do you dwell on trivia to avoid confronting more serious topics? How much of your speech is focused upon your spiritual development?

I say to you,
Do not swear at all.
Do not swear by the heavens—it is God's throne.
Do not swear by the earth—it is God's footstool.
Do not swear by your head—
you cannot make a single hair black or white.
Say "yes" when you mean "yes" and "no" when you mean "no."
Anything else is tempting you from the path.

Jesus of Nazareth

Meditation leads to becoming aware. And our words create a large impression of who we are. What does our speech say about us? Does it reveal us as spiritual seekers? Do we use speech to mask how we are really feeling or to avoid the feeling itself? Oh, I'm all right. No problem here. How can we work to make our speech more reflective of how we see ourselves as seekers?

The fourth precept warns against sexual misconduct. Put most simply, and without getting into the many current moral arguments around sexuality, we will label sexual misconduct as behavior harmful to one's self or others. This would cover indulging in risky sexual practices, using sex as power or to attain power, sexual actions as mere expressions of lust, coercive sexual acts (of which rape is only the most serious), sexual behaviors inconsistent with our state in life—a married person having sex outside the marriage.

Is our sexuality connected to our heart and to love? Does it manifest a real concern for the other human being, or is it primarily or even solely for our own enjoyment and pleasure? How do you treat your partner? Is he or she a full human being to you with whom in sex you are communicating on a very intimate level? How do you honor

> The **fruits** of the **spirit** are **love**, joy, **peace**, **patience**, kindness, **generosity**, faithfulness, gentleness, **self-control.**
>
> *St. Paul, Letter to Galatians*

that person as truly other and vulnerably open to you as you are to him or her?

The final precept warns us about intoxicants. Through meditation we seek to change and purify our consciousness. We wish to become more aware and awake to ourselves, our lives, our world. Intoxicants do just the opposite. They may seem to make us more aware, but in truth they dull our senses, leading us into illusion and even delusion.

What is the place of intoxicants in my life? How do I use them? Do I abuse them? These includes alcohol and drugs, but also all substances that intoxicate us. Caffeine. Sugar. Shopping. Sex. The Internet. Food. A person. Television. Gambling. What are my intoxicants? How can I begin to reclaim my freedom from these addictions?

The Community

Meditation seems to be almost an ideal activity done alone. After all, the requirements are that we not be disturbed and that we concentrate upon our own mind. Why should we need a community?

Yet most meditative traditions regard a community of fellow meditators as essential. To become a Buddhist one must embrace not only the Buddha, the Teaching (Dharma), but the Sangha—the community. It is not an unessential but rather an essential part of developing a meditative practice.

The path of meditation is not easy. Yes, at the beginning we may be excited by the newness and the idea that we are going to grow spiritually. But this is a practice that will demand daily attention for the rest of our life. It must carry us through high times and dry times. There are times when it will seem at best a waste of time, at worst a sign of lunacy.

A community of fellows can help us through these times. They keep us accountable. We will practice at times simply not to let our friends down. They provide support. Sometimes they may challenge and teach us. Knowing that we are in this enterprise with others gives us the faith to keep going.

Communal practice aids meditation. As you progress you will begin to notice a difference between practicing alone and with others. When I attended the Buddhist institute, I began to notice that meditation was easier and deeper there than when I was alone. I was not as distracted by thoughts; I

Abu Musa reported the Prophet as saying, **"Believers** are to **one another** like a **building** whose parts **support** one another." He then **interlaced** his fingers.

Hadith of Bukhari and Muslim

seemed to know a deeper calm. This was in spite of the fact that there were thirty other people in the room with the inevitable shifting, coughing, and other distractions. I mentioned this to the teacher who confirmed my experience. Yes, when we meditate together we have a stronger meditation than when we do it alone. Tibetan Buddhists even have a kind of meditation battery; objects charged with psychic energy are placed throughout the meditation hall to aid the students.

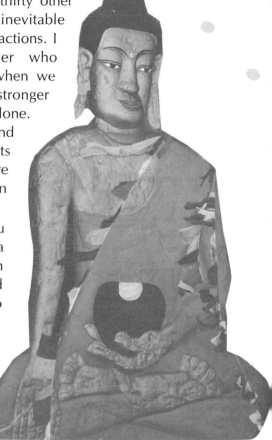

As you build your practice you should begin to search for a meditation community. Where can you go for further instruction and guidance? Who can you learn to call your brother or sister meditator? Who will support you and whom can you support on our mutual journey? The community offers concrete confirmation we are not in this practice for ourselves alone. We are meditating for one another, and for the world as a whole. This journey is much greater than just our own seeking. We are to be here for all others, whether they are aware of our meditation or not.

The Teacher

Do you need a teacher? Ideally meditation is best learned from another human being with experience. However, it is not difficult to learn from a book. In doing so, be careful to pay close attention to the directions, especially cautions against trying too hard, looking for results, expectations, etc. Here a teacher and ideally other students are invaluable. Students can bring up issues and questions that arise from the practice and the teacher can answer them and help improve the practice.

But then there is the question of the guru—a person who claims spiritual authority and is more than a teacher. Gurus are a part of many meditational systems. They are found not only in the East in Hinduism and Buddhism, but in Christianity, Judaism, and Islam. A real guru can greatly speed a student's spiritual progress. He or she can hone in on the student's real issues and problems and save a great deal of time by bringing those issues up rather than waiting for them to emerge during the long course.

But how do you know a guru is the real thing? We live in an area of spilled spirituality. The old traditions had ways of certifying a spiritual teacher. Today almost anyone with enough chutzpah to hang out his or her shingle can pass for a guru. At best a false teacher will hinder your own spiritual journey. Examples of the worst that can happen range from Jonestown to Waco.

Bhagwan Shree Rajneesh, one of the more controversial spiritual gurus of our time, claimed it was one thing to kiss the feet of a statue of Christ, and another to kiss the feet of the Bhagwan. The statue is made of marble and surrounded by millennia of devotion. But it is also buried in millennia of traditions and accretions. Much of the original spiritual charisma is gone. The Christ will not mislead you but he will not shock you or enlighten you either.

The earthly Jesus in his day was another matter. If you kissed his feet you were taking a chance, putting your life on the line. Who knew where he might lead you? The cross certainly does not look that appealing from the earthly side of Easter. He might have lead you to annihilation.

So with the Bhagwan. Kissing his fleshy feet takes courage and risk. You claim him as your teacher. He takes responsibility for your spiritual life. How do you know he will lead you to the truth? To kiss his feet is to open yourself to great spiritual energy. But is he really what he says he is? If he is not he could lead to your undoing. The unsettling end

Approach someone who has realized the purpose of life and question him with reverence and devotion; he will instruct you in this wisdom. Once you attain, you will never be deluded.You will see all creatures in the Self, and all in Me.

Bhagavad Gita

of his Oregon community certainly shows the risks of a guru, just as the subsequent history of the Jesus' or Buddha's disciples reveals the advantages of a true spiritual master.

Intellectual Environment

Meditation is not sufficient in itself to advance us upon a path of spiritual growth. Where are we going? What is the goal of our effort? What are we seeking? For the Christian it will be union with God in Christ—a spiritual marriage. For the Buddhist it will be Nirvana. For the Hindu it will be absorption in Brahman.

Further, what are the stages along the path? What are the obstacles to progress? What kinds of things should we look for? What should we avoid? Meditation attached to a spiritual tradition can guide a person toward spiritual maturity. When considered on its own, it is incapable of leading us far and can, if used wrongly, cause considerable harm.

So an intellectual component is essential to any real spiritual practice. We need to learn a tradition. What are the authoritative writings, the Scriptures? Who are the trusted teachers of the past? How am I to understand my journey?

On the other hand, it is all too easy to allow the mind to run away with things. We can become caught up in reading books like this and never actually start practicing. Practice and practice alone is of supreme importance. Reading a book may guide you in your practice, but it can never take the place of it.

Six Classics of Meditation

Hinduism

Yoga Sutras of Patanjali. Core text of meditation (which is a branch of yoga) for the traditions of the Indian subcontinent. See Web: http://reluctant-messenger.com/yoga-sutras.htm

Buddhism

Anapanasati sutta. Sutta on the Mindfulness of the Breath—a basic text in Theravada Vipassana Meditation. See Web: http://www.accesstoinsight.org/canon/majjhima/mn118.html

Calm and Clear by Mipam. Classic text on introductory meditation in the Tibetan Tradition. See: trans. Kenneth Dowman, Dharma Publishing, 1987

Taoism

Secret of the Golden Flower. Presents the practice of turning the mind around. See: trans. Thomas Cleary. Harper San Francisco, 1993

Christianity

The Cloud of Unknowing. Serves as the basis for Centering Prayer. See Web: http://www.ccel.org/u/unknowing/cloud.htm

Way of the Pilgrim. The basic text in the Orthodox Church for the Prayer of the Name or Jesus Prayer. See: trans. Helen Bacovcin. Reprint, Image Books, 1978

Exoteric and Esoteric Teaching

Most traditions have two kinds of teaching: the first, exoteric teaching, is meant for all the members of the community. Esoteric teaching is secret, or hidden, and is given only when the pupil is ready to receive it. We Westerners are often drawn toward such secret teachings. And today, with the spilling of spiritual traditions into the common arena, it is not hard to find such esoteric teachings. They were originally hidden not because they contain some great code or secret but because the majority of people were not capable of receiving them, would not know how to put them into practice, and would likely pervert them.

A good example of exoteric teaching can be found in the sayings of Jesus. Jesus seems to have believed that there was no need to keep such teachings hidden. When a person was ready for them. they would reveal themselves. And so it is today. How many Christians really understand or practice turning the other cheek? How many actually work on resentments and anger? In other traditions these would be hidden practices. They are powerful. To practice such things pulls the plug on life as we know it. As G. K. Chesterton once said, "Christianity has not been tried and found wanting, it has been found difficult and seldom tried."

The search for secret teachings is by and large a waste of time. We need to start where we are and we are not ready for such advanced practices. We need to believe what most traditions promise: do the work you have to do now. In other words, work with some ways of meditating found in this book. When you are ready, a teacher will appear to take you to the next step.

5. Taming the Ox

I hold on to the whip and rope;

> *never letting go.*

He may stray off on some dusty road.

> *But devotedly trained, he becomes docile;*

unfettered, he follows his master.

Comment: Hold the reins tight, beware of any doubt.

Use all the helps available: meditation, teachers, community.

Delusion is a dusty road.

Part Two

Meditation
in the
Spiritual
Traditions

exploring a great spiritual practice

chapterfive

Why are SpiritualTraditions Important?

In spite of what some new age teachers might suggest, meditation is not completely neutral. It is not true that if you simply meditate you will find enlightenment. Meditation is employed by various spiritual traditions to lead the seeker along the path. But there must therefore be some path—some wisdom—that guides the meditator.

Today Buddhism, which has quite developed forms of meditation, is often presented as of secondary importance to the meditation itself. Yet Buddhism does not advocate neutral meditation. It has what it calls a "view," which colors and guides the path of the meditator. Parts of this view include the teachings of no soul, no perduring human essence, and no creator God:

everything is impermanent. Such views at least on the surface go against much Western Spiritual teaching, which emphasizes just the opposite: there is a human person, there is God, and although transient, creation is not a simple passing away.

In the beginning you may be drawn to meditation as a simple way to relax and find peace. But any serious engagement should lead you to a spiritual tradition within which you can continue to practice and be guided toward the truth.

You may want to reexamine the tradition of your youth. You may have rejected it simply because your spiritual education stopped at an early stage. Although you continued to grow in intellect and in other studies, your understanding of your spiritual tradition remained at a childlike level. Although all traditions try to educate their children in their wisdom, you cannot expect them to provide the child with the fullness or the breadth of the tradition. It is as though you stopped learning mathematics with the division tables and assumed that was all there was to know. What about algebra, trigonometry, geometry, let alone calculus? Do not sell your tradition short. Take time for a second look.

Of course, being so potent, religious traditions can and do succumb to the quest for power. They can hurt as well as heal. Perhaps hurts in your past make you loath to return to the tradition that wounded you. It may be easier to find solace from another source. But remember, eventually encountering and healing the various wounds of our past forms part of any spiritual journey. Otherwise we will always have a partial and biased outlook.

The great mythologist Joseph Campbell grew up Catholic. He was an altar boy. And for much of his life he was blinded to the graces of the Western or at least Christian tradition. He would claim that all Christians took their teachings literally, while Tibetan Buddhists regarded their mythology metaphorically. Now the truth is that a peasant is a peasant. And a scholar is a scholar. There is more correspondence between the Tibetan and Christian peasant than between the Christian peasant and the Christian scholar.

There are levels of teaching in any spiritual tradition worth the name. If we are blind to that we may never find the wholeness we are seeking. At the end of his life, Campbell made peace with the Catholic Church.

We will examine the various major spiritual traditions and the role of meditation, as well as the kinds of meditation within them. This is not to say that in the present climate syncretism is not possible. The different traditions have great gifts for one

Meditation is the practice of a few, but it is at the very center of all the spiritual traditions. . .

another. Certainly Jews and Christians have greatly benefited from Buddhist meditation teachers. Buddhism has reawakened their own forgotten mystical and contemplative traditions. The forms of meditation are not necessarily tied to just one spiritual tradition. For example, Hinduism and Buddhism share many of the same meditative practices. And there is no reason why a Christian may not practice yoga, provided he or she understands just how such a practice may contribute to the Christian path of holiness and salvation.

Meditation is the practice of a small minority in every spiritual tradition. Even Buddhism, which exalts meditation to a very high position, is still composed of householders, lay people, who do not have time for the meditative path in this lifetime. Instead, by supporting the monks and nuns who beg food from them, they contribute toward a further incarnation when they will have the opportunity to meditate and enter the monastery. Meditation is the practice of a few, but it is at the very center of all the spiritual traditions—it is the vehicle common to all the paths which bring us to our goal.

Beginnings of Meditation

The beginnings of meditation are lost in the mists of prehistory. We do not know just how long ago humans began to explore techniques of meditation which would enable them to enter more deeply into reality. But we can make some guesses. The discovery of fire is one of the great milestones of human progress. Haven't we all felt the seduction of a campfire—staring into the flames? Seeing shapes, losing ourselves in the constantly shifting dance of the flames; we are entranced.

Or perhaps ancient hunters developed meditation during the hunt when they had to remain silent and disappear for long periods. Other scholars suggest that psychedelic drugs such as Soma in India or psilocbic mushrooms aided the evolution of our consciousness. When these substances disappeared we found other ways to achieve these states of consciousness through meditation and other ascetic practices. All we know for certain is that meditation entered into human experience early on, before recorded history, and has been a part of our story ever since.

Primal people today may shed some light on our ancient ancestors, but this is not a provable hypothesis. After all, these peoples have probably progressed just as literate peoples have. Who are we to say that they remained at the same stage of development over centuries?

But these indigenous peoples do show us the universality of seeking after higher states of consciousness. The psychologist Abraham Maslow added the desire to expand consciousness to the other human drives such as food, sex, and preservation. And another psychologist, Andrew Weil, has shown the many ways in which we strive to achieve this "high," which includes the many forms of meditation.

Indigenous peoples today use dance and chanting, sweat lodges, vision quests, fasting, vigil, psychoactive substances, and all the traditional ways to achieve altered states of consciousness. And they also often assign a role to a special person, the shaman or medicine man or woman. This person is gifted with the ability to pass back and forth between the worlds and is initiated and instructed how to make the journey by the elder shaman. They will preserve and pass on the wisdom and secrets of the tribe. The shaman guides the people, delivers them from danger, heals their sicknesses.

We can see examples of such shamanic behavior in the ancient Greeks. Socrates seems to have been possessed of a *daimon*—a genius who guided him. The Greeks journeyed to Eleusis to visit the oracle where through the use of psychoactive substances, ritual, vigil, and fasting the priestess gave them advice.

6. *Riding the Ox Home*

I mount the ox,
  and slowly turn toward home.

My flute's voice sings to the
evening,
  beating time, my heart fills with
  joy.

All who hear know I am one who knows.

Comment: The struggle is
over. No need to hold the
reins.

Practice has become a natural
activity. I see clearly now.

exploring a great spiritual practice

chaptersix

The Traditions of India

We immediately have a problem with the very name, Hinduism. What is Hinduism? It is not a coherent religion such as Buddhism, Judaism, or Christianity. Hinduism refers to the religious traditions of the Indian subcontinent which are not one of the two great other native traditions—Buddhism or Jainism—or another religious tradition, such as Islam or Christianity. Thus, Hinduism is what is left after we subtract the other more defined religions. But Hinduism also includes elements from all those traditions.

Buddhism did not supplant the native traditions to become the religion of India because Hinduism was able to incorporate many of Buddhism's key insights into its own traditions. The forms of Vedanta popular in the West today, through such teachers as Aurobindo, Krishnamurti, and Paramahansa Yogananda (the teacher of Christopher Isherwood and Aldous Huxley), are actually a Hindu

From the unreal lead me to the Real! From darkness lead me to the light! From death lead me to immortality! OM.

Brihadaranyaka Upanishad

response to Buddhism. Similarly a Hindu, hearing the Christian gospel, would not necessarily convert to Christianity, but might add Jesus to the Hindu pantheon and incorporate Christian teachings into his own tradition.

This exchange between traditions has given rise to Pravhavananda's commentary, *The Sermon on the Mount According to Vedanta.* In politics, Jesus' teaching of nonviolence was first taken up by Gandhi as a way of really acting in the public sphere and helped achieve Indian independence before being adopted by Dr. Martin Luther King, Jr. in the civil rights movement. This melding of traditions continues today with two Christian books from a Hindu perspective: Abishiktananda's (Sanskrit for "Light of Christ") book *Prayer* and Bede Griffith's *River of Compassion: A Christian Commentary on the Hindu Bhagavad Gita.*

No definite process makes one a Hindu—no baptism as in Christianity, no taking refuge as in Buddhism. And within the tapestry that is Hinduism we can find all sorts of seemingly conflicting beliefs and practices. Some Hindus believe in nonviolence; while others are quite violent. This is true in other religions as well, but in Hinduism the variety is a given. A Hindu is a person who does not deny being a Hindu.

We might say that Hindus agree upon the revelatory meaning of the Vedas—the most ancient scriptures, which serve as the foundation for all subsequent Hindu manifestations; however, this would not be true in the sense that Christians accept the revelatory meaning of the Bible. Many Hindus will never even read the Vedas and may believe in things not contained in them or even disagree with them. The Vedas are really more a symbol for Hindu unity than an agreement on the meanings of these texts.

Similarly, what attracts Westerners interested in meditation to Hinduism are really a few key movements within the Hindu spectrum. So we will direct our attention to these movements.

When Westerners think of Hinduism they immediately think of yoga. But we must expand our image of yoga. It conjures up people twisting into strange and difficult positions, holy men sleeping on beds of nails or walking over coals. While these activities are part of yoga for some people, there are many different yogas, and only one—*hatha* yoga—has to do with the postures so familiar in the West. Other key branches of yoga are *karma* yoga (the yoga of work), *bhakti* yoga (the discipline of devotion that includes the Hari Krishna movement), *jnana* yoga (the discipline of knowledge and the study of philosophy), and *raja* yoga (the yoga of meditation).

Yoga and Body Prayer

Hatha yoga—the yoga or the asanas or postures—is a great help in establishing a meditation practice. Many forms of meditation do very little with the body other than establish a posture for meditating. The postures of hatha yoga are meant not primarily as physical exercise, but as a way of meditating with the body. In the asana it is most important to be fully aware of the body and the breathing that goes along with maintaining the posture.

We Americans are pretty out of touch with our bodies. A spiritual practice, if it is to be at all holistic, must take account of the bodily dimension of our being. When the Tibetan teacher Tarthang Tulku Rimpoche came to the States and began teaching Americans, he realized that we were not really connected to our bodies. The body stabilizes our practice; if it does not, we tend to float away. We become detached. Real spirituality is supposed to help us live in this world, in this life. What good is it if it simply removes us to some far off cloud land where we can bliss out? To help us he

A posture assumed by a **Yogi** must be steady and pleasant. When command over the postures has been thoroughly attained, the effort to assume them is easy; and when the **mind** has become thoroughly identified with the boundlessness of **space,** the **posture** becomes **steady** and **pleasant.** When this condition has been attained, the **Yogi** feels **no assaults** from the pairs of **opposites.**

Patanjali

developed a discipline out of yoga, Tibetan medicine, and Buddhist tradition—Kum Nye—which enables people to enter into the bodily dimension of experience and establish the ground for future growth. Here is a sample exercise:

Take a seated position with your hands on your knees.

Relax your belly.

As you inhale raise up your shoulders
*   toward your ears as high as possible.*
*   Shift your hands as necessary.*

When you reach the extreme position relax
*   while still holding the shoulders high*
*   and you may be able to raise them a bit higher.*

Allow your neck to sink down between the shoulders.

Hold your breath a little and imagine the back of your neck
*   as if it were fresh and warm like a happy baby.*

Now as you slowly exhale rotate the shoulders back and down,
*   keep your awareness in your neck and the back of your spine.*

Keep the hands and arms relaxed.

Continue to rotate the shoulders forward up and down
   three or nine times.
   Try to take at least a minute for each rotation.
Then find a place in the rotation
   where you can comfortably change direction
   and make three or nine rotations the other way.
When you are finished, continue sitting for five to ten minutes,
   aware of whatever is happening in your body and mind.
Allow the sensations and feelings to expand.
Be directly present to them.

Hatha yoga helps people do the same thing as Kum Nye—become grounded in the body so that it can serve as an anchor for meditation. To gain some sense of this yoga try this basic posture sequence: the Salute to the Sun. This is a series of separate asanas joined together in a routine.

Practice. . . .

Salute to the Sun

Stand up straight, feet together, knees straight but not locked.

Now allow your arms to move out and upwards to the sides as you inhale.

*Join the palms over your head
and bring the hands down in front of your face
in a prayer position as you exhale.*

Inhaling, reach the hands up and over your head again.

Bend just slightly backwards.

*Look upwards toward your hands.
Do not overdo this stretch.*

Then return to upright with hands stretching upward.

As you exhale begin to bend forward.

Stretch out with the arms as you bend downwards.

Keep going until your hands touch the ground in front of your feet

*(or stretch as far down as they can. Then, if necessary,
bend your knees to allow the hands to touch the floor.)*

The feet and hands should form a straight line.

*Inhaling, stretch your left leg backward
so that the toes and knee rest on the floor.*

*At the same time raise your head
and feel the stretch all along the back and the leg.*

*Exhaling, move your right leg back so that it joins the left,
at the same time lift your left knee off the floor.*

*You are now in a plank position
similar to the start of a push-up.*

*Inhaling now drop the knees, chin, and chest to the floor
in that order.
When you are lying on the floor
hold your breath
and begin
The Cobra asana:
Raise your forehead, nose, chin, neck
and then shoulders from the floor.
Your hands are still in the same position
as when you touched the floor with them.*

Try to lift using the back muscles
rather than pushing with the hands and arms.
As you lift up look upward with the eyes
as far as possible
and allow the chin to jut outwards and
upwards.
Hold the position for a moment
and then come down, in the reverse order
of how you went up.
Your forehead should be the last to touch the floor.

During the posture, keep the legs together and as relaxed as
possible.
It is not important how far you stretch
but simply that you extend yourself a little.

Now as you inhale
bring the left foot between your hands.
The right leg remains stretched out behind
with the knee on the ground.
Again stretch by looking up
and feeling the stretch all along the back.
Then, exhaling, bring the right leg forward
to join the left between the hands.

*Inhaling, stretch the arms upwards over the head
  and once again stretch backwards just a little.*

*The head follows
  so that in the extreme position
  your eyes are looking upwards and a little backwards.*

*Exhaling, allow the arms to come forward,
  palms joined together in a prayer position.*

*As the arms lower in front of the body
  allow the hands to gently touch
  the forehead, the mouth, and the heart.*

*Allow the arms to descend until they come to rest
at your sides.*

In learning this sequence, break it up into the various postures—forward bend, backward leg stretch, plank position, cobra, etc. Again, it is not important to do the stretch perfectly at first. Do what you can with a gentle exertion. Do not pull the body into a stretch. Rather, see how within the posture you can let go of tension and sink into the posture—this is especially the case with the forward bend and the cobra. Do not push or pull, but relax and let go. If it is too much to do the breathing at first, learn the posture and add the breathing later.

The Sun Salute provides a stretch to every part of the body and once the body is stretched it is able to relax more.

So the Salute is a perfect prelude to sitting meditation as well as a meditation in itself. If you have trouble meditating because you cannot sit still, consider yoga or one of the other body meditation disciplines.

Since yoga has become so popular in America today it has developed many different forms. Many of them are not really geared toward spiritual practice but have become a part of our fixation on fitness and physical prowess. When searching for a yoga teacher, find one that keeps the spiritual dimension. If you feel exhausted or in pain at the end of a session you are probably doing one of the nonspiritual variants of yoga or trying too hard. You can check with the American Yoga Association for help in finding a teacher (www.americanyogaassociation.org).

Iyengar is the most famous yoga teacher in the West today. His form of yoga is so popular that already his students are divided over how it should be practiced. His school employs blocks, ropes, and other tools to help the student get into and maintain postures.

Transcendental Meditation (TM) consists of meditation on a mantra in the same way as other mantra meditations, such as the Jesus Prayer. In TM, however, the mantra is specially imparted to the disciple during an initiation ceremony. This initiation is quite expensive. True, if you invest a couple hundred dollars to receive your mantra you are more likely to persevere than if you receive one from a book. But whether the special mantra has any truly extraordinary power has yet and probably never will be proved.

The Hare Krishna movement also uses a form of meditation. Here the disciple chants a simple prayer throughout the day. This movement has certain cultish characteristics. A cult may provide tremendous energy to bring to the practice, but it does so at the expense of individual freedom. This is a question that needs to be pondered by every spiritual person.

Buddhism

Buddhism began in the fifth century B.C.E. when the Indian Prince Gautama left his easy life to search for true fulfillment. He visited various teachers and then decided to sit under a Bodhi tree until he attained understanding and enlightenment. Once enlightened he began to preach his discovery of the Middle Way by proclaiming four noble Truths:

1. Suffering exists
2. Suffering arises from attachment to desires
3. Suffering ceases when attachment to desire ceases
4. Freedom from suffering is possible by practicing the Eightfold Path:

   Right View   Right Thought

   Right Speech   Right Action

   Right Livelihood   Right Effort

   Right Mindfulness   Right Contemplation

Four Noble Truths

First, that suffering is a fact of life is not as negative as it seems at first sight. It simply points out that there is a basic unsatisfactory quality to our existence. We will never find true happiness and contentment in this present state. Second, this suffering is caused by attachment or desire. We want to have things, to possess things. And we also want to push away certain things. Whether it is desire or hatred it is attachment, and this attachment creates suffering. What is to be done? The third truth claims that liberation from suffering and the restitution of human freedom is possible. How? The fourth truth states that human effort toward detachment must involve all aspects of our life in a deeply spiritual way.

The second great insight of the Buddha is that everything is profoundly interrelated. There is no such thing as a separate self-sufficient entity. Everything has causes and is related to every other thing in existence. This is illustrated primarily through the Great Chain of Dependent Origination. Our present mental state is caused by preceding states and in turn gives rise to the next states. And the final state in turn causes the first state setting the cycle in motion again. There are certain points at which one can break the cycle.

The Buddhist teaching spread rapidly throughout India and eventually throughout Asia taking many forms. It died out in India because it was absorbed into the Hindu system and the Muslim invasions wiped out Buddhist institutions and schools.

Today Buddhism exists in two basic forms, Theravada and Mahayana. Within the Mahayana are found Zen Buddhism (which we will explore in Far Eastern traditions) and Vajrayana or Tantric Buddhism.

Theravada Buddhism, the smallest of the two forms, is found in Southeast Asian countries such as Burma, Cambodia, and Thailand. (Vietnam is primarily Zen.) It means "The Way of the Elders" and is the most conservative form of Buddhism. The scriptures are in Pali and the goal is to practice meditation so that one becomes enlightened.

> **When this exists, that comes to be; with the arising of this, that arises. When this does not exist, that does not come to be; with the cessation of this, that ceases.**
>
> *Cycle Dependent Origination*

Some people confuse Theravada with Hinayana Buddhism. Hinayana was the first manifestation of Buddhism and was overtaken by the Mahayana. Hinayana was concerned with individual salvation, whereas the Mahayana preached the way of the Enlightening Being. Theravada is similar to Hinayana but has also developed through the course of time. While the Mahayana emphasizes emptiness and compassion, that does not mean that they are not present in the Theravada tradition.

And just as might a **mother** with her life
Protect the son that was her **only child,**
So let him then for every living thing
Maintain unbounded consciousness in being,
And let him too **with love for all the world**

Maintain unbounded consciousness in being

Above, below, and all round in between,

Untroubled, with no enemy or foe.

And while he stands or walks or while he sits

Or while he lies down, free from drowsiness,

Let him resolve upon this **mindfulness**

This is **Divine Abiding** here, they say.

But when he has no trafficking with views,

Is **virtuous,** and has perfected seeing,

And **purges greed** for sensual desires.

He surely comes no more to any womb.

Metta Sutta

No matter which school or culture, the essence of becoming a Buddhist is taking refuge in the teacher, the teaching, and the community. This triple refuge vow said three times, makes one a Buddhist:

I go for refuge in the Buddha,
I go for refuge to the Dharma,
I go for refuge to the Sangha.

Triple Refuge, Vipassana Meditation

Vipassana Meditation

Most modern Theravadins who meditate practice Vipassana. This meditation combines the two basic Buddhist meditation practices: stopping and seeing, or calming and clearing. The first object must be to stop the incessant activity of mind. We need to calm the mental chatter. When the mind is calm we can begin to observe the way it works. In such a way we are able to free ourselves from our mental patterning and begin to perceive reality as it is. We experience the three characteristics of reality: that it is impermanent, that it is not satisfactory, and that it does not have a self. It is one thing to try to understand these concepts philosophically, but another entirely to experience their truth. That is the aim of Vipasana, or insight meditation.

While there are separate practices for calming and then for insight, vipasana combines the two into one. There are many kinds of calming and insight practices found in the various Buddhist schools. But Vipassana is recognized by all of them, Theravada or Mahayana, as the essential form of meditation.

Practice...

Begin by taking a meditation posture.

Focus upon the breath. Entering. Leaving. Simply notice it.

Choose some place to focus—perhaps at your nostrils,
or in your diaphragm, the choice is up to you.

Between the breath choose some part of the body to focus upon
so that you have a focus at every moment.

When something else comes into consciousness
identify it.

Pain. Thinking. Boredom. Planning.
Don't spend too much time labeling -
this is only a device to keep the mind
focused on the meditation.
Keep the labeling simple and on the surface -
do not search after deeper meanings.

Simply be aware what is happening in this moment.

Books on Insight Meditation

∼ Rosenberg. *Breath by Breath: The Liberating Practice of Insight Meditation.* Shambala, 1998.

∼ Goldstein. *The Path of Insight Meditation.* Shambala, 1995.

∼ Kornfield. *A Path With Heart: A Guide Through the Perils and Promises of Spiritual Life.* Bantam Doubleday Dell, 1993.

After practicing attention upon the breath for a few months, turn your attention next to the body— notice particularly the various sensations in the body, be attentive to the whole body, settle into the body and fully experience it. As usual, when something comes up simply notice and name it and return to the body. Subsequent practices shift the focus to the feelings and finally to the mind.

The Mahayana is found throughout the far East: China, Japan, Korea, Vietnam and Tibet. It is known as the "Great Vehicle." The great insight of the Mahayana is the truth of *sunyata*: "emptiness" or better still "openness." This teaching is attributed to Nagarjuna, a philosopher whose teaching questions all attempts to define reality in terms of human language or thought. Openness means that there is nothing in the sense of a separate self-contained entity. This is not to be confused with nihilism, which claims that nothing truly exists. Rather the Buddhist believes in an existing reality but denies that there is any separate, self-substantial subject or object within that reality. All is in a state of constant flux, arising and disintegrating, combining and coming apart.

Liberation comes from stopping the attempt to grasp. This insight into the radical emptiness of all being is the definition of wisdom.

> O Shariputra, form is no other than emptiness,
> emptiness no other than form;
> Form is exactly emptiness, emptiness exactly form;
> Sensation, conception, discrimination, awareness are
> likewise like this.
> O Shariputra, all dharmas are forms of emptiness, not
> born, not destroyed;
> Not stained, not pure, without loss, without gain;
> So in emptiness there is no form, no sensation,
> conception,
> discrimination, awareness. . .

Heart Sutra

In early Buddhism people sought their own liberation. But gradually they began to perceive that since all things are interconnected it would be impossible for one part of reality to be liberated unless all of reality was liberated. This gave rise to the Boddhisattva (Enlightening Being) who takes a vow not to enter Nirvana until all beings are able to find liberation. Such a train of thinking leads to the importance of compassion which for the Mahayana is of equal importance with wisdom—the openness of all being.

Innumerable are sentient beings: we vow to save them all.

Inexhaustible are deluded passions: we vow to extinguish them all. Immeasurable are the Dharma Teachings: we vow to master them all. Infinite is the Buddha's way: we vow to fulfill it completely.

Boddhisattva Vow, from Zen tradition

Wisdom without compassion is useless. And the opposite, compassion without wisdom, is totally ineffective. So, for Buddhists, an important part of practice involves remembering why they are practicing: to relieve the suffering of all beings. They do this at the beginning, when they dedicate the fruits of the practice to others. This teaches them on a profound level the importance of compassion. They hope to alleviate the sufferings of others and lead all beings to liberation.

Compassion Meditation

This is a visualization practice. If you have trouble visualizing, it is enough to pretend you are doing so. Practice will strengthen the ability to visualize as well as the ability to meditate. There is no substitute for practice. Never give up. The meditation should take about twenty minutes.

Practice. . . .

Take up your meditation posture.

Take a few deep breaths to center yourself.

First focus upon yourself.

   Think about your good points.

   Overlook your negative qualities.

   Feel compassion for yourself.

   Truly wish only happiness and love for yourself.

   You are a good and loving person.

   You are working for the happiness of all.

Be compassionate toward yourself.

Now visualize three people in front of you :

   a friend to your right,

   a stranger in the middle,

   and an enemy or someone you cannot stand on your left.

First, concentrate upon the friend.

Examine your feelings toward that person.

This should not be difficult.

Give love and friendship to this close friend.

This helps generate the compassion
which we shall next extend to others.

After a short time move on to the stranger in the middle.

Realize that he or she wants only happiness.

Whatever they do, good or bad,
they do because they believe it will lead toward happiness.

Give this person now love and kindness.
Wish that they might find the happiness they are seeking.
And imagine the person benefiting from your wish.

Now move on to the enemy to your left.

Forget your issues with this person for a moment.

Try to give some understanding and even love to that person.

Now realize that the stranger or even your friend
could do something that would make them your enemy.
They could cheat you or hurt you.

Now look at the enemy
and realize that this person may become your friend in the future. They might help you.

*Now look at your friend and feel
your love and compassion.*

> *And try to hold this
> feeling as you move
> back toward your
> enemy.*

> *Remember he or
> she, like you, only
> seeks happiness.*

*Can you feel just a little
love and compassion for
this person?*

*Try to realize that all four of
you*

> *are simply looking for love and
> happiness.*

Now leave the individuals behind

and allow your love and compassion

> *to spread out into the world.*

First offer it to your friends and family,

> *and to those in the immediate area.*

*Next expand the compassion to include your town, your
country.*

*Allow the compassion to expand until you include the entire
world.*

Do not force the process.

If you cannot feel compassion
simply imagine you are doing so,
that is enough for a successful practice.

When you are ready gently come out of the meditation.

You might wish to pray the following prayer:

May I be a bridge and a ship for those
who want to cross the water.
May I be an island for those who seek one,
and a lamp for those desiring light,
May I be a bed for all who wish to rest,
and a hand for those who need a help.

Buddhist Prayer of Compassion

The Mahayana has taken many shapes in the different cultures into which it was introduced. Zen is the most popular form in the West, but we are mistaken concerning the true state of Buddhism in Asia. Westerners think of Buddhism as a meditating religion and indeed it does propose meditation as a key way to attain liberation, but it does not follow that most Buddhists meditate. In Japan only 20 percent of Buddhists practice Zen.

The majority of Buddhists belong to the Pure Land School, which teaches that if one devotes oneself to the Buddha Amida by praying his mantra, one will be reborn in a Pure Land where one will have the opportunity and resources to achieve enlightenment. The mantra used is: *Namu amida budtsu.*

Mahayana Buddhism embraces hundreds of schools and traditions, which all incorporate the two insights of openness and compassion. Unlike various denominations of Christianity each believing that the others are in heresy, Buddhism, at least on the highest level (there is always a human urge toward bias), exalts this infinite variety, as described in the Lotus Sutra, chapter 5:

> *The Buddha is like a cloud.*
> *The Buddha appeared in this world just as a large cloud rose.*
> *Although he equally expounded the Dharma*
> *to gods, people, and all living beings,*
> *they understood his teachings differently,*
> *but they are still able to vitalize the teachings*
> *depending on their abilities, characters and specialties.*
>
> *In this world, there are many different races,*
> *culture, customs, and education.*

The Eternal Buddha accepts the differences
and applies different teachings to each individual
in order to maximize their understanding.
It sounds like discrimination,
but it is real equality and compassion.

Finally, there is the Vajrayana, the Diamond Vehicle, or the Tantric forms of Buddhism found today among Tibetans and in Japan, where it is called Shingon. This is part of the Mahayana and does not differ through any special teaching. It does, like Zen, emphasize the doctrine of the Buddha Nature, that everything is of Buddha Nature: empty of self-being. Since all partake of Buddha Nature, one is already liberated, one simply does not know it and has not had the experience.

The Tantra incorporates many practices from Indian Tantric traditions where it was born and evolved. It uses mantras as words of power that are able to access the energy of liberation and so shorten the journey. It also uses many other means such as visualization and the infamous sexual yogas to shorten the journey.

Today, due to the occupation of Tibet and the displacement of its people, many tantric teachings have been made public. This is unfortunate, for these teachings in their purity are extremely powerful and should only be undertaken with a qualified guru as guide.

On the other hand, one may use certain mantras such as, *Om mani padma hum*, or the Padmasambhava mantra, *Om*

Ah Hum Vajra Guru Padma Siddhi hum. These mantras are in Sanskrit rather than Tibetan; their power is believed to reside in the words and sounds themselves. They do not have any specific meaning. And although the power resides in the sounds, Tibetans do not chant them with their original pronunciation. For example, *padma* sounds like pay-ma and *hum* is pronounced hung. So the pronunciation is not inviolable.

Other traditions, particularly in India, consider the pronunciation extremely important. Still other traditions such as the Jesus Prayer (discussed below) place the power in the name itself, not on its form. Tibetans chant alone or in a group or recite silently. After one hundred thousand repetitions, one is initiated into the mantra and it becomes one's own. To help with the count the meditator uses a strand of prayer beads called a mala.

7. Letting go of the Ox

Riding the ox,
  I arrive back home,
  serene.

The ox is no more;
  at dawn, blissful
  dreaming.

Under the straw roof, I lay
down both whip and rope.

Comment: The ox is no longer needed. We have found ourselves.

Practice no longer involves a goal. Life itself is practice.

exploring a great spiritual practice

chapterseven

FarEastern
Traditions

T he religious experience of China is quite different from other cultures. Westerners may claim that there are three major Chinese religious traditions: Confucianism, Taoism and Zen Buddhism. But these do not function as Western religions do. A Chinese saying claims that when one is born or dies one goes to the Buddhist, when one enters the world one uses Confucianism, and when one is sick or has bad fortune one goes to the Taoist. Sometimes when reading Chinese religious texts it is difficult to ascertain whether they are Confucian, Taoist, or Buddhist. The three do not stand against one another as Christianity, Judaism, and Islam do. Rather, they have throughout history influenced and borrowed from one another. I have waited until this chapter to discuss Zen because it shares much with Taoism and varies greatly from other forms of Buddhism.

Confucianism is a system mainly of ethical relations, which articulates values of family life and the administration of the state. It also incorporates the traditional Chinese veneration of ancestors and engendered a cult of Confucius as the official patron of education and culture. As such it is not a meditative tradition. This is not to say that Confucianists do not meditate but that they meditate as Taoists or Buddhists.

The Way of learning to be great consists in manifesting

the clear character, loving the people, and abiding in the highest good.

Only after knowing what to abide in can one be calm.

Only after having been calm can one be tranquil.

Only after having achieved tranquility can one have peaceful repose.

Only after having peaceful repose can one begin to deliberate.

Only after deliberation can the end be attained.

Things have their roots and their branches.

Affairs have their beginnings and their ends.

To know what is first and what is last will lead one near the Way.

Confucius

There are actually two different faces of Taoism. Westerners are most familiar with philosophical and mystical Taoism as found in the *Tao Te Ching* and the *Secret of the Golden Flower.* But popular Taoism in China before the Communist revolution was largely magical and superstitious dealing in spells; popular Taoism was also concerned with health and hygiene and employed the system of Chinese medicine and the martial arts.

The Taoist sage wants to identify with the great all, the impersonal Tao. To do this he uses meditation and trance. This union leads the sage to become nameless, formless, and simple, while at the same time attaining virtue or power. Through "non doing" he attains everything because he spontaneously unites with nature and finds his original self.

Tai Chi Chuan

Taoist meditation is concerned with the generation, transformation, and circulation of internal energy. Once the meditator has 'achieved energy' (deh-chee), it can be applied to promoting health and longevity, nurturing the 'spiritual embryo' of immortality, martial arts, healing, painting and poetry, sensual self-indulgence, or whatever else the adept wishes to do with it. One result of the Taoist quest is a very long life; the great sages were thought to become immortals.

Much Taoist meditation uses the same techniques as Zen, but it offers us also the martial arts, especially Tai Chi Chuan—a form of movement meditation. It is beyond the scope of this book to teach a form of Tai Chi. It must be learned directly from a teacher. Although there are three official styles, each teacher has such a different variant upon the official forms that sometimes it is hard for the student of one teacher to recognize the postures in another teacher's practice.

If you are interested in pursuing Tai Chi, consult a number of teachers. Sit in on their classes to see their particular form. Choose a form that appeals to you. Some teachers emphasize the martial arts aspect, some the meditative. Again, what are you looking for? I learned the short form from my teacher in ten weeks, meeting once a week. Two friends studied with another teacher and did not begin to learn the actual form until one year after learning the preliminaries.

As a result of the popularity of Tai Chi there are also simplified variants available today. Tai Chi Chih is a series of twenty simple movements which, like Tai Chi, awaken the spiritual energy and circulate it throughout the body. As the West learns more about martial arts and Chinese medicine it is recognizing as well the values of this system and encouraging their implementation.

This simple meditation moves the *chi* or spiritual energy throughout the body. All spiritualities recognize this spiritual energy—in Buddhism and Hinduism it is called 'prana' and in Christianity it is the 'Holy Spirit'—but Taoism cultivates it and directs it to promote both health and spiritual development. While Indian systems speak in terms of chakras or spiritual centers along the center of the body, Taoism names channels running up and down and throughout the body. These are similar to the acupuncture points. In this meditation we will circulate the spiritual energy in an orbit through the major channels.

Circulating the Chi

Begin by taking a seated position in a chair,
    both feet on the floor,
    hands palms down on your upper thighs.

Sit to the front edge of the chair
    so that only a small part of your buttocks are on the chair.
    This will allow the chi to flow more easily and smoothly
        without being obstructed by the chair.

Shut your eyes.

Shut your mouth and allow the tip of your tongue
   to rest lightly on the upper palate, the ridge just in back
   of your front teeth.

Turn your awareness within.

Visualize a pocket of energy in the region of the navel.

Within the pocket visualize a point of golden light,
   clear and bright, pure.

Focus until you feel the energy glowing.
   At first just imagine it doing so.

Allow your breathing to be through your nose.
   It will become light and quiet. Do not attempt to alter it.

Now use your mind to guide the energy
   up your front along the center of your body.

Imagine the energy flowing upward from your navel
   and into your heart and lung region.

Up from the heart, now through the shoulders and into the
neck,
   up the neck and into your mouth.

It travels up the tongue and into the upper palate,
   up the front of your face,
   through the nose and up into your forehead.

Now it achieves the top of your head.

At this point it begins to pour down your back,
down the back of the skull into your neck,
into your back and slowly down your spine to its end,
the coccyx.

Now it begins to come to the front again
up into the genital region and back to the navel.

Continue the circulation. Move the chi slowly.

At first you may simply have to pretend it is happening,
but with practice you will begin to feel the chi
and with further practice it will become
more and more noticeable and powerful.

As with other meditations, when you become distracted and notice it simply return to where you left off, or if you have forgotten where return to the navel. Do not stop the process at any one point along the route but keep the *chi* slowly flowing. The breath will gradually align itself with the *chi*—do not force this. Do not worry about the breath—it will take care of itself. Your only concern should be to keep the *chi* moving slowly. Practice this for twenty minutes twice a day.

Zen Buddhism

■ ■ ■ ■ ■ ■ ■ ■ ■ ■ ■ ■ ■

The third strand of Chinese religion is Buddhism, especially Zen ("Chan" in Chinese). Both mean "seated meditation." Zen attempts to bring the student back to the basic experience of meditation and direct seeing. I have waited until this point to discuss Zen, because it shares much with Taoism and varies greatly from other forms of Buddhism.

Zen has some characteristics which cannot be taken too literally. It relies on oral transmission rather than book knowledge. Zen does not deny the importance of a teacher to guide and especially avoid the many pitfalls along the way. Nor does Zen have no place for books or book learning. It is not anti-intellectual, but with other Mahayana schools asserts it is impossible to express reality in human language and thought.

Emerging Western Buddhism is focused upon meditation but such was not always the case in Asia. There Buddhism developed a huge intellectual and philosophical tradition. Such teaching can become a substitute for real experience and real practice. Zen calls us away from anything that is not direct experience of the real. Ideas and concepts have their place, maybe, but nothing can take the place of actual experience.

This leads the Rinzai school in Japan to use the *koan*—a kind of puzzle—to break through ordinary thinking and open the meditator to the real. The most famous koan is "What is the sound of one hand clapping?" or "What is the shape of your original face?" Given such a *koan* by one's teacher, the disciple meditates upon the answer. Each time one arises he or she returns to the teacher. The answer is not the crux of the process but rather the attempt itself leads the meditator to *satori*—a spiritual awakening.

Oh, I could sing such grandeurs and glories about you!

You have not known what you are, you have slumbered upon yourself all your life.

Your eyelids have been the same as closed most of the time. Whoever you are! Claim your own at any hazard!

These shows of the East and West are tame compared to you,

These immense meadows, the interminable rivers, you are immense and interminable as they.

Walt Whitman, To You

Someone asked Yangqi, "When the **founder** of **Zen** came from India to China, he sat facing a wall for nine years—what does this mean? Yangqi said, "As an **Indian,** he couldn't speak Chinese."

Zen story

Before enlightenment there are the mountains and the carrying of water. During enlightenment there are no mountains, there is no carrying of water. After enlightenment there are the mountains and the carrying of water.

Zen saying

Just because one has achieved *satori* does not mean the journey is ended. At first one only has inklings of this new way of seeing. One must develop it and finally integrate it into everyday life.

The Soto school of Japanese Zen emphasizes the power of "just sitting." Since everything is Buddha nature then what is to achieve? Where is there to go? Taking the sitting posture itself is enlightenment. Naturally it demands many takings of the posture and much meditation to realize this "simple truth."

Practice . . .

This meditation involves just sitting
and being aware of what is going on at just this moment.
This is moment-to-moment mind.
It hears the birds in the trees,
the cars going by,
the planes overhead,
and the children playing outside.
To the clear mind there is no such thing as 'noisy',
it all just 'is'.

Clear Mind Meditation

This meditation, actually the simplest possible form, is not
for beginners. We need to calm the mind first so that we
might be able to begin to simply be here now.

Zen is far from the only form of Chinese Buddhism but it is the most known in the West through its Japanese forms. Unfortunately, a militaristic culture colored much Japanese Zen. If you want to study Zen without the militaristic overlay, look to the Zen of Korea or Vietnam.

8. Ox and Self both forgotten

Ox, whip, rope,
*   me too—all gone.*

Who can grasp the vastness
of the blue sky?

*   How can a snowflake*
*   survive a raging fire?*

The spirit of ancient masters is
manifest.

俱人八
忘牛

Comment:

Beyond all dualities. No outside, no inside, no subject, no object.

No words can express it.

Having become one with self-nature, there is no longer self-nature.

chaptereight

Western
SpiritualTraditions

Judaism

Judaism is a response to the destruction of the Hebrew Temple in Jerusalem in 70 C.E. How could one be an Israelite and keep the ancestral faith with no temple to center that faith? For the Jew, the Torah (Law) became the new temple and the rabbis (or teachers) became the experts in the Law. To live the Law throughout one's life is to recreate the Temple of God in the present day world.

What does it amount to— their expounding the **Torah!** A man should see to it that all his actions are a Torah and that he himself becomes so entirely a Torah that one can learn from his habits and his motions and his motionless **clinging to God.**

Rabbi Leip

Meditation enters the Hebraic tradition around 500 B.C.E. with the appearance of the prophets. The prophets claimed to have revelations from God. Of course this led to the question of true and false prophets, the former naturally greatly outnumbering the latter. They may have used meditative techniques or other spiritual practices to induce their revelations. But whatever they used is lost to history; it was their message that mattered more than their techniques. The most extreme and colorful of these prophets was Ezekiel:

As I looked, a stormy wind came out of the north: a great cloud with brightness around it and fire flashing forth continually, and in the middle of the fire, something like gleaming amber. In the middle of it was something like four living creatures. This was their appearance: they were of human form. Each had four faces, and each of them had four wings. . . . In the middle of the living creatures there was something that looked like burning coals of fire, like torches moving to and fro among the living creatures; the fire was bright, and lightning issued from the fire. The living creatures darted to and fro, like a flash of lightning.

Ezekiel

Such a vision would eventually give rise to the practice of visualizing what Ezekiel saw in order to be initiated into his experience. As in all three western traditions, the central authorities were often skeptical and critical of meditation. In Judaism the technique passed into the hands of the Kabbalists and the Hassidim; it was often forced underground or even abandoned due to hostility.

Sabbath

Harvey Cox has pointed out that the real equivalent to meditation in Judaism is the Sabbath. As in meditation the disciple takes time out each day to simply be, so the Sabbath is one day each week set aside to simply be. To play. To pray. To praise. The Sabbath forms a part of all three Western religious traditions. Often it is neglected in our busy lifestyle. Consider taking up this practice: one day a week to devote to God, your family, simply being. No work, but play is encouraged. Like meditation it is the pause that refreshes, that truly bestows meaning upon the rest of the week. This practice could prove very

Let the words of my mouth, and the meditation of my **heart** be acceptable in thy sight, **O Lord, my rock** and **my redeemer.**

Psalm 19

beneficial to spiritual seekers everywhere. The stores may be open on weekends, but do we have to go shopping?

Meditation is not really a central practice of Judaism. Today many Jews have discovered the practice and have integrated it into their own religious lives. Jews who also look to Buddhism for guidance even have a name—the Jubu—and books that help Jews discover this new dimension of their faith.

Imagination

The fierce power of **imagination** is a **gift** from **God.** Joined with the grandeur of the mind, the potency of inference, ethical depth, and the natural **sense** of the **divine,** imagination becomes an instrument of the **holy spirit.**

Abraham Isaak Kook

Meditation itself is reserved for Kabbala, an esoteric body of thought and discipline. Kabbala, of which there are many schools and forms, employs a number of meditative techniques to bring the person into contact with the Deity. These are secret practices and should only be learned and practiced under the guidance of a true teacher. They have also been limited traditionally to Jewish males older than 40 years of age although today they are sometimes opened to both women and non-Jews.

Whenever possible, **avoid eating** in a **hurry.** Even at home, don't gobble up your food. **Eating** is an **act of holiness.** It requires full presence of **mind.**

Rabbi Nachman of Breslov

Kabbala had a picture of the creation as a great outflowing of the divine sparks from God. These sparks have passed to the ends of the universe and they are lost. The task of the student of Kabbala is to aid in the gathering up of these sparks into God again.

Since these practices are secret I will not discuss them here. Many of the meditations bring the practitioner into a closer, less mediated contact with reality and can safely be practiced by a beginner. The teacher encourages the students to pay attention to all their experience, whatever it might be. Listen to the sounds. See what is before you. Be conscious of what you are doing. We do so much on automatic pilot. Practice being aware and conscious. For the next practice you will need to get an orange. That will be the object of meditation.

Practice. . . .

Begin by simply holding the orange.
   Feel it. Feel its weight. Its mass. Its texture.
   Smell it. Take your time.

Now begin to peel it.
   Slowly. Consciously.
   Be aware of the textures.
   The smells. The sight.

When you have peeled it,
   take a wedge.
   Again be aware of it in your hand.
   See it. Take your time.
   Now slowly taste it.
   Savor it.

Hold it in your mouth before you chew on it.
   Then slowly bite into it.
   Experience the juice as you first taste it.

Eventually swallow it and move on to the next bite.

Continue eating the orange with awareness.
   Enjoy it. This is not work. This is relaxation.
   Savoring.
   Being grateful.
   Participating in the creation of God.

Eating an Orange.

Christianity

■ ■ ■ ■ ■ ■ ■ ■ ■ ■ ■ ■ ■ ■ ■

Christianity was born into a culture, much like our own, awash in spiritual traditions and practices—the Roman Empire. Mystery cults, gnostic groups, and traditions competed with native religions. Even Buddhism was present thanks to Asian merchants on the Silk Road.

Christianity, like Judaism, grew out of the destruction of the Hebrew temple in 70 C.E. when Hebrew traditions had to be drastically reexamined. Religious life could no longer center around the temple and its sects—what would replace it in religious life? For the Christians, Jesus Christ became the new temple and focus of faith. At first these early followers did not believe they were creating a new religion at all. They were simply redefining how to be an Israelite in these new strange times. And Paul, considered by most as the greatest apostle, also opened the church to gentiles who were drawn to the nobility of the Hebrew God. Paul argued these gentiles did not have to adopt Jewish traditions such as circumcision or dietary laws in order to join the church—they only needed to acknowledge Jesus as their savior and be baptized. When the other Israelite communities exiled the followers of Jesus, the Christian Church turned even more fully toward the gentiles and grew very quickly.

Christianity quickly forsook its Hebraic roots and became a Greco-Roman religion. Meditation was usually the province of monks and nuns who left the world behind. The establishment has not always been comfortable with mysticism and has sought in the past to restrict it to these cloistered groups. If the mystic can have first hand experience of the divine, how essential is the institution? So many mystics, particularly in the West and especially in Protestant churches, have been questioned and even persecuted. Both Sts. John of the Cross and Teresa of Avila, two of the greatest Catholic mystics, lived under the shadow of the Inquisition.

For Christians the goal of meditation is to come close to God. St. Athanasius defines the Greek ideal: in Jesus, God became man so that through Jesus man might become God. In the West the image of spiritual marriage dominates. The believer is caught up in the very being of God and enters into the divine union.

The Orthodox Church

There are three major divisions of the Christian Church: The Orthodox Church, Roman Catholicism, and Protestantism. Orthodoxy is the form of Christianity practiced primarily in the Middle East and Eastern Europe, especially Greece and Russia. It traces its roots back to the apostles and broke with the Roman Church in the ninth century. Since then, believing that only the full Church can make major decisions, Orthodoxy has not acknowledged doctrines the western church articulated since the schism.

In the East meditation was carried on in the monasteries and centered around the Jesus Prayer, also known as the Prayer of the Name or the Prayer of the Heart. This prayer was later brought out into the world where many lay people chose to practice. This led to the great classic of the Jesus Prayer, *The Way of the Pilgrim,* in which a layman tells how he was initiated and taught the prayer by his teacher, called a *starets:*

To pray truly means to direct the thought and the memory,

without relaxing, to the recollection of God,

to walk in God's divine Presence,

to awaken oneself to God's love by thinking about God,

and to link the Name of God with one's breathing

and the beating of one's heart.

The Way of the Pilgrim

Practice. . .

The practice of the Jesus Prayer is simple.

Stand before the Lord with attention in the heart,
  and call to Him:
  'Lord Jesus Christ, Son of God, have mercy on me!'

The essential part of this is not in the words,
  but in faith and contrition,
  and self-surrender to the Lord.

With these feelings one can stand before the Lord
  even without any words,
  and it will still be prayer.

Theophane the Recluse

The various teachings about the Jesus Prayer are collected in a volume known as the *Philokalia*. It is currently being published in English and runs to several volumes. Many of the writings are quite advanced and secret but the prayer itself can be performed by anyone from novice to saint.

As with many spiritual practices there are initiations advised. Baptism, the Christian sacrament of initiation, makes a person a member of the body of Christ and gives permission to take up this prayer. Some writers even claim that the Baptism must be the Orthodox form.

The traditional formula of the Jesus Prayer is given above, but the essence of the prayer is the name of Jesus. Indeed, simply the name itself can be used. Other variations are "Lord Jesus Christ, Son of God, have mercy upon me a sinner," and "Come Lord Jesus."

Pentheus (contrition) is an essential component of this prayer. This is not simply a sorrow over our sinfulness. Rather it is the awakening of the profound experience of the creature before the Creator: a feeling of unworthiness, or incompleteness. It is not guilt or masochism, but rather the true awareness of who you are—a creature, flawed, sinful, but also at the same time beloved of God.

Some use a Jesus Prayer strand of one hundred beads to help focus, but piling up repetitions as a sign of progress is not advised. The beads simply help keep the awareness focused upon the prayer. There is no official posture. In some monasteries the monks use very low stools. They sit and then pull their hoods up over their heads to shut out the outside world. But posture is not key. You can pray while standing in line, even while driving. Indeed, it helps to maintain calm in driving situations. It is hard to yell at another driver and pray for mercy at the same time.

One begins the practice by praying out loud. The voice keeps attention focused upon the prayer. After the prayer begins to be a part of you, allow it to fall silent. Continue to pray it silently in your mind. And after a time God will allow the prayer to sink from your mind into your heart. There finally the prayer begins to pray you. Christ enthroned in your heart completes your transformation.

The tradition cautions against visualizing Jesus or generating emotions. This is a prayer that begins in the mind and finds its ultimate place in the heart; it is not the heart of easy emotionalism but the spiritual heart of true love.

The tradition is quite forward against forcing the prayer into the heart. It also prohibits aligning the prayer with breathing in any forced way. Those warnings are a sure sign that disciples did harmonize the prayer with breathing. But without a knowledgeable guide, changing the breath can lead to serious psychological and even physical problems. This is true in any prayer tradition. Allow the breathing to conform to the prayer. If it changes—and it will—let it change. Surrender your control to God. Accept your creatureliness. Allow God to take charge.

Catholicism

T he Roman Catholic Church considers itself the mother Church of Christianity, since it is gathered around the successor of the apostle Peter, the first Pope, as a sign of unity going back to the first days. While the Orthodox acknowledge his position, they are not currently in communion with him and so the one church is split.

The Roman Catholic Church is the largest but not the only Catholic Church. Any church that embraces the early authoritative teachings, like the Nicene creed and sacraments, is catholic—this would include the Anglican-Episcopalian Churches and the national churches, such as the Polish Catholic Church.

In the mother tradition of Western Christianity, as in the East, meditation was generally restricted to monastic life. And even in the monasteries the majority of people were not mystics or meditators. Contemplative prayer was seen as a gift given to only a few. Mystics often came under harsh scrutiny. St. John of the Cross and St. Teresa of Avila may be Doctors of the Church today, but another great mystic, Meister Eckhart, is only now after hundreds of years being accepted as a legitimate teacher.

However, one popular form of meditation was considered appropriate for everyone. Surprisingly, this turns out to be a quite complex practice—the Rosary. While the monastics prayed the one hundred and fifty psalms each week, lay people, being illiterate, could not hope to do so. St. Dominic created the Rosary as a way that everyone could join in the Prayer of the Church.

The Rosary

While for most of us the Rosary calls to mind a specific Catholic practice, many kinds of prayer beads are found in different spiritual traditions and within the Catholic church itself. The rose is the symbol of Mary, the mother of Jesus, and so the Rosary is a bouquet of spiritual roses for her. The common Catholic Rosary is more correctly called the Dominican Rosary promoted by the followers of Dominic in the Middle Ages. But there is also a Servite Rosary, and others in use. There are even variations on the way one prays the Dominican Rosary.

Nor are prayer beads isolated to the Catholic tradition. Orthodox Christians use beads or knotted rope to pray the Jesus Prayer. Today there are Protestants who have taken up the

More on the Rosary and Prayer Beads

A Rosary for all Christians

See Web:
http://www.ecumenicalrosary.org/

Traditional Rosary

See Web:
http://www.familyrosary.org/main/rosary-how.php

I also recommend *A String and A Prayer,* by Eleanor Wiley and Maggie Oman Shannon, a book dedicated to the topic of prayer beads–how to use them and how to make them.

prayer and adapted it to their own tradition. They might replace the Hail Mary with a more suitable Protestant prayer. A variant suitable for all Christians, called the ecumenical Rosary, can be found on the web.

Muslims use prayer beads to pray the one hundred names of God. Hindus and Buddhists use prayer beads (called *malas*). The way the prayer bead strands are constructed and used in the different traditions varies. While the Muslim rosary has thirty-three beads, the Hindu and Buddhist *malas* have one hundred (although the Buddhist *malas* are actually one hundred and six beads). The common bond is a string of beads used to ground the body in prayer (you pray one prayer on each bead) and sometimes to keep count of the number of prayers. Tibetan Buddhists believe that a person should perform one hundred thousand repetitions of a mantra in order to be initiated into it and in order for it to unfold its power for the person praying.

Stations of the Cross

Another popular form of meditation arose in Catholicism related to pilgrimage. Christians longed in the middle ages as they do today to visit the Holy Land and its sites. The Franciscan community developed a way to accomplish this sacred journey In essence. Catholic Churches have the fifteen Stations of the Cross represented in small pictures or statues usually running around the sides of the sanctuary. Sometimes a church or a shrine will place the stations outside. Each Station presents an incident from the passion and death of Jesus. The meditator moves from station to station and pauses to reflect upon the incident from Christ's passion and what it reveals to him or her.

See Web: http://www.cptryon.org/xpipassio/stations/

Other forms of visualization

Christianity is rich in visual meditation, since it is based upon the stories and events in the life of Jesus. One of the most popular disciplines of Christian meditation today are the Ignatian Spiritual Exercises. These were developed by St.

Ignatius of Loyola during the Counter Reformation of the fifteenth century to form men in the spirituality of the Jesuit community. The full exercises take one month and are performed under a spiritual director on retreat. For that month the person maintains silence except for a once-daily talk with the director. Each exercise leads the meditator into a story of Jesus in order to encounter and be transformed by the experience.

Ignatius did not create the meditation procedure but rather brought elements together into a new whole. One begins by picturing a biblical scene and entering into it. Allow the different senses to guide you into the story. What do you see? What do you hear? What do you smell? What do you feel? What do you touch? Enter the story. Take on a character. What does this character's experience teach you about the story?

Ignatius wants to use all means to engage the meditator in the story. Through the meditator's own experience God will touch him or her. Breaking down the different sensoria combines with other means on the retreat—the new surroundings, the silence, the being lifted out of our ordinary life—to help God break through our traditional defenses to offer us new insights and grace.

Today the exercises are available for all people. They can be experienced on weekly or monthly sequences or even done at home as a year long process. Many spiritual directors have also been taught Ignatian spirituality and will employ his method in their direction.

This free flowing visualization is at the opposite extreme from Tibetan deity-yoga. In this, the disciple visualizes a quite complicated image, or *mandala*, in extreme detail to the point that the image serves as a gateway into reality. The visualization does not end with a perfect replication of the image. The disciple then goes on to imagine him or herself as the deity. In doing so you gain the graces and powers of that deity. This should only be done under the guidance of a teacher.

The power of images to transform are attested to by all traditions. In Christianity, Dante admits to starting his Divine Comedy with an experience of being lost at the midpoint of his life. He finds fulfillment and salvation through a massive visualization of Hell, Purgatory, and Paradise. Dante's vision is so exact that people have been able to map his journey precisely.

Protestantism

The Protestant movement criticized many elements of the Catholic Church including her mystical traditions. Meditation frequently came under fire as well as the whole idea of monasticism. In spite of this bias, mystics appeared among Protestants. They were often considered heretics and ended up creating their own sects and churches. Among these are Jacob Boehme, John Wesley, George Fox, and Emmanuel Swedenborg, and farther out from the

Dost thou call the steeple-house the Church? The Church is the people whom God has purchased with His blood and not the house.

George Fox

institutions the great English poet and illuminator William Blake.

Today many Protestants are reevaluating mysticism and meditation. They are part of the current spiritual awakening in our culture. The ecumenical monastery in Taizé, France has helped to reintroduce and foster meditation, liturgy, and mysticism for all Christians today. Similarly, the Centering Prayer movement crosses denominational boundaries and even reaches out to non-Christians. This practice is found in the eleventh century spiritual classic *The Cloud of Unknowing.* It has been revived today by Basil Pennington and Thomas Keating. The name Centering Prayer grew out of a series of retreats offered at St. Joseph's Abbey in Spencer, Massachusetts, in the 1970s. From there it has grown internationally.

Centering Prayer

Centering Prayer is a simple method that sets up the ideal conditions for resting in quiet awareness of God's presence. This way of prayer is alluded to in many passages in the Old and New Testaments. The Greek Fathers referred to it as *monologion,* "one-word" prayer. The desert father Abba Isaac taught a similar form of prayer to John Cassian who later wrote of it in France, transmitting it to Benedict of Nursia. By the sixteenth century the prayer form largely went out of use in favor of more discursive modes of prayer.

Practice. . .

Sit comfortably with your eyes closed:

Let yourself settle down.

> *Let go of all the thoughts, tensions, and sensations you may feel and begin to rest in the love of God who dwells within.*

> *Take up a love word and let it be gently present,*

> *Supporting your being to God in faith-filled love.*

When you become aware of thoughts, or as internal sensations arise,

> *just take this as your signal*

> *to gently return to the word,*

> *the symbol of your intention to let go*

>> *and rest in God's presence.*

If thoughts subside and you find yourself restfully aware,

> *simply let go even of the word.*

Just be in that stillness.

When thoughts begin to stir again, gently return to the word.

At the end of your prayer time, take a couple of minutes to come out of the silence—even if you don't feel you need it.

Many people find this a perfect time to internally express to God their thanks and to pray for others in need of God's grace.

The word you choose is up to you. Common choices are "God," or "Jesus," in which case it becomes a form of the Jesus Prayer. But people also choose words such as "love" or "peace." The Relaxation Response, a modern secular offshoot developed by Harvard psychologist Robert Benson, recommends a word such as "one." You do not want to choose a word charged with emotion. Choose a fairly neutral word. The prayer does not encourage you to bring emotion into it.

Practice this for twenty minutes, twice each day.

Islam

Islam is the last of the world religions to appear and considers itself the final revelation from God. It confesses that "There is no God but God and Mohammed is His messenger." *(La ilaha ill-llah, Muhammad-un Rasulu-llah.)* Mohammed in the seventh century C.E. received revelations from God, which eventually became the Qur'an—the Holy Scriptures of Islam. These scriptures are not equivalent to the Christian or Jewish Bible. The Bible is regarded as God's revelation through human mediation. Muslims believe the Qur'an to be the actual word of God. Therefore it should be approached in the original Arabic, and really occupies the same position that Jesus Christ holds for Christians—the very Word of God.

We need to be aware when considering Islam that we may have many prejudices against this religion. It is the least understood religion in the West today, associated as it is in many minds with terrorism, the subjugation of women, or a rejection of the West and modernity. While Islam encompasses these elements, they do not define the religion itself or every follower. Just as Westerners tend today to idealize Buddhism, so do we demonize Islam and neither prejudice helps toward true understanding. To call the Qur'an or Islam a religion of terrorists is to repress our own tradition's past. How is Samson, who brings down a Philistine temple and in so doing kills himself and hundreds of innocent people, not a terrorist?

The Five Pillars are demanded of every Muslim. One must recite the daily prayers (*salat*) five times during the day. And one must fast (*sawm*) during the season of Ramadan. One  must make the pilgrimage (*hajj*) to Mecca at least once in one's life. One pays the religious tax (*zakat*) to aid the poor. And one engages in holy struggle (*jihad*), which is not war against infidels although it has been perverted into that, but rather struggle against whatever within you resists God. These pillars sanctify a man's terrestrial life and enable him to live and to die as a person destined for beatitude. But these rites themselves are not limited to their outer forms. They possess inner dimensions and levels of meaning as well.

The goal of the Muslim, in the words of the Qur'an, should be, "A soul at rest" (89:27). We reach such a state depending upon our relation to God. The more we turn our attention to God, the more God bestows inspiration upon us. So God helps us pass through the various stages of spiritual growth until we ultimately reach that pinnacle of sublimity so desired by God.

Sufism

Islam is not primarily a meditative tradition but it contains an esoteric mystical core known as Sufism. The Sufi esoteric schools teach various meditation techniques including the whirling dervishes. While teaching the technique of the dervishes is beyond the scope of this book, we can explore meditation in movement through dance as a way of praying through the body.

Dance Meditation

In dance we allow the body to lead us and to teach us. Dance is not only "speaking" but "listening." We listen to the body and its movements, its sensations, its waves. We allow our body permission to express ourselves beyond words and thoughts, and the body puts us in touch with ourselves and our world. Too much meditation is an attempt to leave the world behind, but a true spirituality does not want to forsake the world so much as to reclaim it.

Practice. . .

This meditation may be done alone or in a group. If you use music, keep it simple and rhythmic. Focus on the rhythm with your dance.

To begin, find a space for your dance.

> *This is sacred space and the dancing is sacred time—*
> *space and time*
> *out of the ordinary.*

Enter the space and the dance consciously.

> *Notice the transition from the busy outer world*
> > *to the dedicated dance space.*

Start with deep, slow breathing.

> *Bring your thoughts to a stillness.*

When you are ready, begin to dance.

> *Remember this is not a performance but a prayer, a meditation. Allow the body to guide you.*
> > *Let go of expectations and self-consciousness.*
> > *Be attentive to what is happening.*

What are you feeling? What emotions arise?

Feelings are of great importance here. Be aware of them.

Resist analyzing or judging. If your mind rebels, let it play itself out.

Keep to the movement.

Give the body its chance.

Repeat movements over and over again.

This is a kind of ritual that always includes repetition.

The repetitions will help your body disclose to you

what it is feeling and sensing.

After the dance stops, enter into silence.

The meditation is not over.

Don't rush things: this is the most important part of the dance.

In the silence you can absorb the qualities evoked by the dance.

Many Sufi schools claim to be followers of Jesus, not as the Son of God, but as a supremely important teacher of God's love. Some scholars believe St. Francis of Assisi was taught by such Sufis while he stayed in the Middle East. Certainly many strands of Franciscan spirituality are similar to Sufism: the use of teaching stories, the place of song and poetry in praising God, the centrality of love over all.

The Sufi's goal is self-discovery and he or she embarks on a journey that strips the covering of the self to approach its inward reality. Many methods are used to assist in discovering the inner meaning of reality. Some find purification, abandonment of the world, the resistance of temptation, and reliance on the will of the Divine to be a way to discover reality. Others find meditation, prayers, and service as ways to find salvation. The goal, not the means, is of supreme importance.

For some the goal becomes annihilation in God. The "I" is empty. Only God is real. It is said that the Prophet's love for the Divine was so powerful that it is not easy to separate the lover from the Beloved Allah.

I wonder at this You and I
You are all there is
And I am all annihilated.
There is an I
No longer exists.
Mansur al-Halaj
We searched a while for the Divine
Within the depth of our illusions
Looking there to find His signs
In the Beings of "you" and "I".
When love appeared
"You" and "I" were dissolved,
And found no more need to follow signs.

Moulana Shah Maghsoud,
20th century Persian Sufi

Invocation of God

The central practice of Sufism is the Invocation of God or *dikr*. Repeat over and over the divine name whenever you can recall it during your day. It is a practice of remembering— remembering who you are, a creature, and whom you are made for, God. One can choose the Arabic word "Allah" or one of the one hundred names of God.

Let your invocation be the all-embracing Name,
which is Allah, Allah, Allah, or if you so wish, Huwa,
Huwa, Huwa; and do not violate this remembrance.
Be careful lest your tongue pronounce it
while other-than-He is in your heart.
Let your heart be the one who utters,
and your ear the one who is attentive to this invocation
until the 'speaker' emanates from your Self (sirr).
When you feel the emergence of the Speaker within you
through the invocation,
do not abandon the spiritual condition
wherein you find yourself.

Hadith of the Prophet

9. Returning to the Source

To return to the source—a false step!

Better be blind and deaf from the start.

Sitting in the house,

unconcerned with things outside—

the river flows quietly, the flowers are red.

Comment: Truth is without beginning.

Be still and know.

Self-consciousness no longer distorts the world.

The Royal Road of Spiritual Growth

exploring a great spiritual practice

chapternine

TheOxHerding
Pictures

Just what is all of this work of meditation for? Where are we headed? The different spiritual traditions provide responses to these questions. But to conclude this introduction, let's look at two maps that can serve as guides whatever the spiritual tradition. The two maps arise from quite different sources and do not cover quite the same territory. The first map, the Ox Herding pictures, is ancient and charts the course of the practice of meditation itself. The second map comes from current scientific inquiry and points out the various stages along the path toward our goal as spiritual beings.

One. Searching for the Ox

Dante began his *Divine Comedy*, "In the middle of my life, I woke to find myself lost in a dark wood." From there he begins a journey in search of his estranged self (Hell), of his current self (Purgatory), and ultimately his true self (Paradise). The boy represents the search for our true self—the ox.

First comes waking up to the question. Many never even wake enough to ask it. When did you first ask the question? This moment is known as the "first stirring of the heart" and is precious and beautiful. Of the millions alive today, only a few will realize this moment. And of those very few, fewer still will come to realize that the answer is not lost or outside, but within our own being. All beings are truly Buddhas. Having lost sight of this truth we search desperately everywhere but within.

What was life like before you woke up? What were your goals? Why didn't they satisfy? What made you ask this question and start to search for the ox? Did many previous searches go astray? Did certain things hold out a promise only to disappoint? Wealth? Power?

When we first awake to the question we may seek outside for the answer. We look to philosophy, science, the occult. But the more we seek outside, the more estranged we become from our true self.

So long as we feel that the ox is far off we wander in vain. Happiness is something that is out there, in the future, unattainable the way I am now. Yet in truth the search for the ox is very similar to the search for the glasses perched on your nose all along.

Dante found himself lost in a woods where the ox lives. How do we get to the woods? We are already there—the woods are our lives now. Here we begin.

Two. Discovering Footprints

When we embark upon this search we begin to see tracks. The more carefully we look we find tracks everywhere. Consider, we are looking for the real. How can the real not be everywhere? Indeed, the real is all there is.

Others have been upon just this search. And they have much to tell us. We begin to read books, go to lectures, listen to spiritual teachers. They all have sought the ox.

But there is a danger here. We have not even seen the ox yet. Some of us remain stuck here, looking for footprints. Books and lectures are the footprints, not the ox. He will only be found through practice, through meditation.

Zen says that people at this stage are trapped in the theoretical. No matter how well they understand, no matter how brilliant their research, they are still here finding the tracks. Thomas à Kempis said he would rather be able to experience "contrition" than be able to define it. Only experience is liberating and experience is gained only by practice.

Three. Glimpsing the Ox

The young man sees the ox's tail sticking out from the trees. First sighting! It is real! There IS an ox! Zen calls this moment *kensho* but it is not restricted to Zen or to meditation. It can and does occur anytime, anywhere. We have all experienced it, although we may not have known it as such. Such *kensho* may have led us to embark upon the search in the first place.

Abraham Maslow, creator of the famous hierarchy of needs, calls them "Ah Ha!" moments, or "peak experiences." Suddenly, usually with no warning, you find yourself totally in the moment. It can occur during sports, while making love, playing music, witnessing a sunset. In that moment the small "I" disappears for a few seconds: there is no barrier between yourself and the real. All simply is, and it is good. As soon as one becomes conscious (or should we say self-conscious) of this, it disappears.

"On a branch sings the nightingale," the poet says. The nightingale's song symbolizes this moment. Many Zen masters first found spiritual awakening through sound. Mumon (1113–1260) attained *kensho* on hearing the sound of a great drum. Kogyen was raking in the garden when a rock flew off his broom and struck a bamboo tree with great force. The "whack" woke him up, dissolved the boundaries between him and the real. He experienced the true self.

But we have merely glimpsed the ox. We really haven't seen him yet. Zen calls this third stage the initial opening. We are far from our goal. It may be tempting to think, "Now I've got it. I've seen the light." To see the light and to live in the light, to become the light, are not the same.

Who could draw that great head, those majestic horns! This moment is beyond words. It is beyond thought even. A painting cannot capture the ox. It is alive. Spontaneous. Once we have glimpsed this inexpressible reality we must forge ahead.

Four. Seizing the Ox

Having glimpsed the ox, we now practice with determination. We seize this beast. Grab it by the tail! Now the fun starts. He jumps, bucks, and runs off to the plateau, covered by the mountain mists.

Meditation is not easy. We are in for a long struggle. Who is the ox? Our own true nature. For years it has been deluded in the world. Naturally, it is untamed.

When we begin to meditate we begin to experience just how uncontrolled our mind is. The Hindu tradition describes it as the monkey-mind. It runs off after every little distraction. To be harsh on it does little good and probably much harm. What to do? Learn patience. When it wanders, go after it. Grab hold of it again and return it to the meditation. No use getting upset. Forget becoming angry. This is it: the real work: spiritual transformation.

Ultimately you and the ox are one and the same. As Pogo, Walt Kelley's cartoon character, used to say, "We have met the enemy. And it is us." And it is quite unreasonable to be engaged in a constant struggle with your very self. But that is the path. You must ride out the ox's energy. Sooner or later it will calm down and be tamed.

Five. Taming the Ox

The boy walks down the road leading the ox behind on a rope. Some teachers consider this the most important picture. It speaks of our key experience of meditation. Instead of just glimpsing we must tame the ox.

It is one thing to see the ox, another to seize it. But we cannot stop there. How will we tame it? The rope and the whip symbolize our spiritual tradition. These are instruments for ox taming. They should not imply cruelty to ourselves (the ox). They represent discipline: they help keep the ox on the path. Otherwise it will wander into the dusty roads—the outer world of illusion we wish to leave behind.

As our practice deepens, a spiritual tradition guides us on those dusty roads. Of course, first there is the temptation to go back to our old ways and views. This is a long hard journey. We look back in nostalgia as did the ancient Israelites to the flesh-pots of Egypt. From this vantage point on the journey, they look appealing even though we know that they enslaved us.

But the dusty road also represents enlightenment. We may become swayed by special experiences: we may see visions, experience powers—what the Buddhists and Hindus call *siddhis*. These are very enticing and distracting. When a student approaches a Zen master to excitedly tell him that during meditation he sees the Buddha, the master tells him,

Someone once asked **St. Teresa** of Avila if it wouldn't be wonderful if the sisters were granted **spiritual gifts** such as levitation. She replied, "It would be better if they could scrub the convent floors with **charity** for their sisters."

"Next time you see the Buddha, kill him." This is a distraction from our true journey. A teacher and tradition keep us focused on the narrow path.

How do we devotedly train the ox? We must train from the heart. Buddhism seems primarily concerned with the mind—after all meditation is mind work. Not true. For the Buddhist, as for the Christian like St. Theresa, the key organ is the heart. Our meditation should gradually soften and purify our heart. When we have our experience approved by a spiritual teacher, and reach a stage that most people come to with great difficulty, we are tempted to become inflated: "What a great meditator I have become." DANGER! All our hard work is at risk; we could be worse off than before we began. Only strenuous and continuous training softens the heart. We gradually see that what we are doing is not for ourselves, but for the world. This is the true direction in which we want to go.

Six. Riding the Ox Home

I t would seem that the work is done. The boy has tamed the ox and now rides it home while playing his flute. There is no more need for the reins or the whip. This ox does what it is supposed to do.

At this point we realize our everyday experiences as the content of the enlightened mind. The ideas of subject and object, inside and outside, good and bad begin to dissolve. The extraordinary is the ordinary. We are fully one with the ox. But we are not yet at the end of the journey.

It is tempting to remain here. It is pleasant and happy. It would seem that the work is done. But to do so leads to the sickness of clinging to this experience at an even deeper level.

Seven. Letting Go of the Ox

T he boy has reached home and is sitting down. Where is the ox? Who knows? This is a very different state: previously the boy searched, saw, grasped, tamed, and rode the ox. Here, now: no action. He simply is.

The whip and reins are put aside. No longer necessary. I once studied meditation with a Tibetan guru. He taught us to sit up straight, place our hands on our knees, etc. But during meditation, when I looked, he would be slumped over with his head on his chest. He looked asleep. But no, he was in deep meditation. He had reached the stage when meditation is the most natural thing in the world. He could do it anywhere, in any shape, anytime. No need for the guidelines we still had to cling to.

Now are for us no entanglements or snares,
Nor a bit of egoism left.
Now is all distance annulled, nor are curtains drawn between us.
Thou art mine, I Thine.

Adi Granth, Bilaval

In truth it has been this way since the beginning. The ox was only a means to realize this stage. After all, the ox was our true nature. But it took all this effort to finally realize it. Buddhists point to the moon. It is always there but often obscured by clouds. Once the clouds pass away there is the moon shining as it has all along.

Eight. Ox and Self Both Forgotten

The circle now is empty. Buddhist "emptiness" or *sunyata* does not mean that nothing exists. Rather there are no boundaries between things. Everything is ultimately open to and interconnected with everything else. There is no ox, no self, no whip, no rope, no hut. All are one with the all. Nor is there anything to attain. Enlightenment—this Buddha nature—is present here and now. Our minds are clouded and we cannot perceive it. Once we start to conceptualize it, it remains a thousand miles distant. Here all concepts vanish. We live in pure simplicity. Even thoughts of ourselves are no longer present.

God must be very I.
I very God,
so consummately one that this he and this I are one 'is',
in this is-ness working one work eternally. . .
God's being is my life,
but if it is so,
then what is God's must be mine,
and what is mine God's.
God's is-ness is my is-ness,

and neither more nor less.
The just live eternally with God,
on a par with God,
neither deeper nor higher.
All their work is done by God
and God's by them.

Meister Eckhart

Zen speaks of "falling away of body and mind." You have forgotten yourself, forgotten all others, forgotten everything. There is only one circle without any substance whatsoever. For a Buddha there is no enlightenment, no Buddhahood; samsara and nirvana are one. Praise and blame are the same. To reach this stage you must not "linger where there are buddhas," which means to dwell on concepts such as buddha, *kensho,* enlightenment. Drop everything.

The blue sky is vast and empty. Here is the true nature of reality. You cannot communicate it. You can only experience it. When you realize this you make present again the spirit of the masters.

Nine. Returning to the Source

S ome series end with the eighth picture, but that is not truly so. Everything already completely expresses its Buddha nature. The water flows. The flowers are red.

It has taken an enormous journey of great difficulty to reach this state, which superficially seems to be exactly where we were before we began. All of our work has led us only to the discovery that all we really had to do was "give up." What we have at this stage, who we are at this stage, is "nothing special at all."

Gozu Hôyû was a man of high virtue,
whom people respected deeply.
Even birds praised his virtues,
fetching and offering him flowers.
But later on, after he came to great enlightenment
the birds stopped bringing flowers.
As long as people extol you as a great person,
you are not real.
An enlightened person does not stick out.
The birds fail to spot Hôyû Zenji,
because he turned invisible to them,
as he became nothing special.

Zen story

Is the journey then useless? We may feel that it is not worth it, if we are only going to land back where we started. Some spiritualities promote this kind of lazy enlightenment. "You are already enlightened." True. But only by significant struggle can we truly experience this. It will not come simply by sitting on your cushion, pretending you are already there. You convince yourself that all striving is of no use. This is called "inactive Zen," and it is a particular temptation today. Yes, the journey is to end us where we started. Yes, the journey is nothing special seen from the other side. But between here and that other side comes great struggle.

Ten. In Town With Open Hands

What is enlightenment? A Zen saying: "When I sit, I sit. When I eat, I eat." As simple as that. Simply be here now. Live in the present, spontaneous, alive, in touch. The boy is now a grown man coming to the market place. He has no thought for what others are thinking of him: Clothes ragged, face smudged, I smile.

This final stage has nothing to do with miracles or special powers. Again these may come. Do not be distracted. A student once approached his teacher, excited that during practice he saw dragons and buddhas. "Don't worry," replied the teacher. "They will go away."

The old man offers his purse to a young boy. The end of the spiritual path is not self promotion. There is no separate self to promote. The real goal is the liberation of all beings. May all enjoy the freedom that is the true nature of reality. The Buddha said, "All lands are my land; and all the living beings in those lands are my children." What we have been given, we now give away in turn. Only this sharing truly matters.

chapter**ten**

Meditation:
Walking the
Labyrinth

The labyrinth is an excellent symbol of our spiritual journey. First, it is not a maze that is a puzzle. Caught in a maze, you try to find your way out. The labyrinth is a tool for meditation. There is only one path and there are no dead ends or wrong turns. You begin on the edge and walk to the center; then you turn around and follow the path out to the edge again.

This walking meditation is a form of pilgrimage. People take pilgrimages as a means of spiritual renewal, whether the old medieval pilgrimage to the holy saint's tomb, the Muslim *hajj* to Mecca, or our ancestors' search for a new life here in the new world. The pilgrimage itself is holy and sacred. The journey will change us, transform us, renew us. So the

Sources for Labyrinths

A good source may be in your hometown. Contact a local Catholic Church, monastery, or cloister, or the theology department at your local college. They may know if there's a labyrinth in your area, and if there's someone who can guide your first experience.Alternatively, you may wish to check these on-line sources:

The Labyrinth Society,
    www.labyrinthsociety.org
Veriditas ™,
The Labyrinth Project,
    www.verditas.net
and for personal labyrinth tools, see the offerings at
    www.ispiritual.com
    www.labyrinthproducts.com

labyrinth is a symbol of that sacred journey.

Labyrinths have been around for more than four thousand years in almost every spiritual tradition. They are in old cathedrals, in gardens, and today are being built as vehicles for self exploration and growth. To do this meditation you must first find a labyrinth. A little work on the computer may help you find one nearby.

There are many approaches to the labyrinth. Today, labyrinths are being used for reflection, meditation, prayer, and comfort. Each person's walk is personal. How one walks and what one receives differs. Some use the walk to clear the mind and center. Others bring a question or concern. The time in the center can be used for receiving, reflecting, meditating, or praying, as well as discovering our own sacred inner space. What each person receives may be integrated on the walk out. Your walk may be a healing and very profound experience, or it may be just a pleasant walk. Each time is different.

Practice . . .

Clear your mind and become aware of your breathing.

Find the pace your body wants to go.

Walking toward the center, let the path quiet your mind.

From the entrance to the goal is the path of shedding or "letting go." Release and empty yourself of worries and concerns.

When you reach the center,
    take time for illumination,
    reflection,
    or meditation.

At the center there is illumination, insight, clarity, and focus. Here you are in a receptive, prayerful, meditative mood. Take your time.

As you walk back out,

be strengthened for your return into the world.

The path out is that of becoming grounded and integrating your attained insight.

It is being energized and making what was received manifest in the world.

10. In Town With Open Hands

Bare chest, bare feet,
I come to the marketplace.
Clothes ragged, face smudged,
I smile.
No need for miracles,
I touch dead trees and they
blossom.

Comment: I am
hidden in the
world.

I have no adornments
or pretensions.

I enlighten those around me.

chaptereleven

A
Modern
Map:
Integral
Psychology

The ox herding pictures came out of a meditative tradition. Our chief means of investigating the world today is science. What does science have to say about meditation and its effects on us? Immediately we run into difficulty. Modern science requires objectivity. Only what can be measured is open to investigation. Meditation seems to be one of the most subjective activities imaginable. True science has been able to chart brain waves, blood pressures, and other externals during meditation, but this is hardly the core a meditator would claim for his or her experience. Traditional science stops dead in its tracks.

Ken Wilbur, one of the key synthesizers of consciousness, calls for science to expand its boundaries. Many traditions claim that if one practices in such and such a way, such and such a result will occur. Is not this objective evidence of what is an ultimately interior and subjective experience? Why can it not be taken into consideration? So Wilbur has gathered together information from the various modern and traditional

spiritual psychologies to see what they can tell us about the meditative journey. Surprisingly, without any influence upon one another, the various psychologies present a fairly consistent picture, which we will now explore.

Wilbur's synthesis is vastly rich and detailed. The following brief tour cannot hope to do it justice. Nor has he limited himself to just one map. Some are general, some specific. We will explore a simple map of his system. No matter which spiritual tradition, Wilbur's work is of great help and benefit in understanding both science and spirituality today.

The study of consciousness is the study of evolution. Our consciousness today is not what it was at birth, at three, at five, or at other periods of our life. Nor is the average stage of consciousness today what it was in the time of early homo sapiens, or the Egyptians, or the early Greeks. Consciousness evolves; it develops—historically and individually. Wilbur's map traces that development, which we have made culturally as well as individually.

Archaic-Instinctual

People are conscious even before birth. Through hypnosis, psychedelic drugs, and meditative recall, we can access these experiences. Such consciousness is undifferentiated. We are conscious but not conscious of anything. There is no such thing as me and the other, subject and object. All is one. All our needs are supplied. This is timeless Eden, before any history has occurred.

With birth we move from the womb into the world. Slowly we become aware of needs. We get hungry and are not automatically fed through mother's umbilical cord. Now a teat nourishes us and at times that teat is not available. We are still at a pre-temporal level, ruled by our alimentary canal—feeding and eliminating. That is our world.

Historically and culturally, this is the level of survival bands who forage for food and shelter. At this stage one is still very dependent upon habits and instincts just to survive. We see this level in the first human societies, newborn infants, senile elderly, mentally ill street people, starving populations, the shell shocked. It forms about 0.1 percent of the adult population who has 0 percent of the power in the world today.

Little by little, wean yourself.
This is the gist of what I have to say.
From an embryo, whose nourishment comes in the
blood,
move to an infant sucking milk,
to a child on solid food,
to a seeker after wisdom,
to a hunter of more invisible game.
Think how it is to have a conversation with an embryo.
You might say "the world outside is vast and intricate.
there are wheat fields, mountain passes,
and orchards in blossom:
At night millions of galaxies,
in sunlight friends dancing at a wedding."
Ask the embryo why he, or she, stays cooped up
in the dark with eyes closed.
Listen to the answer:
"There is no 'other world.'
I only know what I've experienced.
You must be hallucinating."

Rumi

Magical-Animistic

This stage is dominated by sense consciousness—what we see, hear, feel, taste, smell. We are moving from the previous states of fusion to the emergence of the self and the first self to emerge is the body—the physical. We learn to differentiate ourselves from the *pleroma*, what is not us. If I bite the blanket it does not hurt. If I bite the thumb it does. A major step forward in consciousness!

Historically, consciousness at this level is involved in magic, as is the child. "Step on a crack, break your mother's back." Break a mirror, seven years bad luck. Primitive humans would draw a picture of the animal which they would then hunt. Killing the animal in the drawing enabled them to kill it in the actual hunt. We also find this level today in Third World settings, gangs, athletic teams (crossing yourself before the toss), corporate tribes, magical New Age beliefs, and astrology. It encompasses 10 percent of the population and has 1 percent of the power.

Power Gods

The two year old's "No" comes with the emergence of language. And once the child has language, it can begin to transcend the simply present world. It can plan for the future. It can begin to delay or control its present bodily pleasures and actions With language, it begins to enter the world of symbols, time as past, present, and future. It is no longer dominated by instinctual demands. The self is beginning to differentiate itself from the body and emerges as a mental, verbal being. The self emerges as an ego distinct from the tribe. What about me?

This stage is seen in feudal kingdoms, Saddam Hussein, James Bond villains, soldiers of fortune, frontier mentality, wild rock stars, the terrible twos, and rebellious youth. It comprises 20 percent of the population and wields 5 percent of the power.

Mythic Order

H ere the ego is reigned in by the society. We live under the rule of an Order or God. There is right and wrong, a code of conduct. To violate the rules brings strong punishment. To do good brings great reward. Law and order rule.

We can see this consciousness today in Puritan America, Confucian China, totalitarianism, religious fundamentalism (Christian, Islamic, whatever), the Boy Scouts and Girl Scouts, the moral majority, patriotism, the idea of an "axis of evil." It includes 40 percent of the population and assumes 30 percent of the power.

Scientific Achievement

A t about age seven, the child begins to be able to operate upon itself and the world around it through concepts. Then, in adolescence, consciousness begins to differentiate itself from the verbal mind. It can operate upon thought itself—it can think about thinking.

In this stage science begins to emerge. The world is a rational machine with natural laws, which can be learned and manipulated. This consciousness forms the basis for corporate states.

We see such consciousness in the Enlightenment, middle classes around the world, market capitalism, the Cold War, materialism, liberal self-interest. It contains 30 percent of the population who wield 50 percent of the power.

For many this seems to be the end of the road—a mature and healthy ego—but it is only about halfway on the journey as the spiritual traditions understand it.

The Sensitive Self

Until now the self has been identified with the egoic mind. That mind lives in a body that it to some extent can control, and that body lives within a world. At the Sensitive level the self begins to transcend the mind. It can begin to think beyond language. It integrates into the psyche the various elements, which on the egoic level are still separate; it integrates the shadow into itself.

The self can see beyond its own culture or history to other cultures and histories, which it can critique and try to integrate into a world culture. The self here is transverbal and transcultural, but it is not yet transpersonal— it has not yet transcended the ego, although it is beginning to intuit that possibility.

This Sensitive realm occupies the forefront of evolution in our culture today. Examples includes deep ecology, postmodernism, liberation theology, World Council of Churches, Greenpeace, animal rights, ecofeminism, post-colonialism, political correctness, human rights issues, multiculturalism. It embraces 10 percent of the population who control 15 percent of the power.

On all these levels the process is pretty much the same; only the content of what is processed changes. The self, at any level, finds a higher-order structure emerging in consciousness. As this happens, the self ceases to identify with the lower structure and begins to identify with the emerging structure. It transcends the lower structure and now is able to work on that lower structure from the higher structure.

The baby begins to use language to articulate its demands, where before it could only express emotion. What happens to the lower structure? Ideally it is integrated into the higher level. Unfortunately, many things can happen on this royal road. People become stuck at various levels. They may repress rather than integrate the lower levels. They may be frightened of what they experience and fall back to a lower level in defense.

Not all people in our society share the same level of consciousness. Democrats tend to be sensitives—the bleeding heart liberal—while Republicans have to contend with mythic types like the Christian Coalition. It is not that one is wrong; all are necessary stages. Consider the damage done through not giving children a good sense of the mythic level as they mature today; they revert to the power God of the rebellious teenager. All levels are necessary but they are levels, not permanent dwellings.

The process can be further damaged if the person or culture does not successfully negotiate the transformation. This is where psychosis can occur. For Wilbur, the current Baby Boomer (Sensitive) disease of refusing to acknowledge any need for hierarchy can be dangerous because, lo and behold, there is higher and lower, better and worse. Not all religion is bad. Not all religion is mythic level. And to think so spells trouble for the overall journey.

Finally, there are ways in which we think we are engaging in real transformation but we are truly only rearranging the deck chairs on the Titanic. Transformation involves moving out of our current apartment and into an apartment on the next floor, quite different from our present habitat. Translation, on the other hand, is simply redecorating the present apartment. Too much modern spirituality is the latter. Transformation is hard and painful. It involves changing our life, our thoughts, and our actions. Translation is simply learning to say the same thing in a different way.

Any description however exalted is inevitably a human one,
and because of this difference in kind
can never be accurate or adequate.
If we say that God is 'great' or 'most high',
or a person is 'good'
we use words which can only be properly understood
in a human context,
words which distinguish 'you' from 'me,'
and each of us from the next man.
Manifestly we cannot speak of Deity like that. . .
God cannot be great or high or personal or good
in our sense of the words.
He is so much more than these
that we speak more truly when we say
that he is none of them,
and is more worthily described negatively than positively.
When the mind faces Him. . . it enters a cloud of unknowing.

The Cloud of Unknowing

Veiled by ignorance, The **minds** of **man** and **Buddha** Appear to be **different;** Yet in the realm of Mind Essence They are **both of one taste.** Some- Time they will meet each other In the great **Dharmadhatu.**

Milarepa

Subtle and Causal Realms

At this point we enter the transpersonal realm. The self now realizes that the individual is but a part of a larger whole. These are the stages of the mystics and they are beyond most of our present experience so there is no real use in differentiating among them here. We can briefly say that the first stages—the subtle in Wilbur's categories—are those in which the self now begins to realize it is larger than the body-mind it inhabits. That body-mind now becomes integrated into a larger structure. Here the self perceives its connection with the deity and becomes integrated into the deity. Some use the image of the "mystical marriage" between the self and God.

Beyond this lies the causal realm—more explored by Eastern traditions—where the self actually comes to identify itself with God. As the Upanishad says, "Thou art that." It is the Buddhist entering into Nirvana where no trace is left. It is not that one becomes extinguished or that there is only a void, but that all is part of the All and apart from the All is no thing. Obviously the population here is quite small and the corresponding power minuscule except in the hands of a leader such as Gandhi or Martin Luther King, Jr. Even then it is almost inevitable that what the person at this stage says and does will be misread by those at lower levels. Consider the inability of disciples to understand what the master truly means, whether that master be Jesus Christ or Buddha.

Where one sees nothing but the One,
hears nothing but the One, knows nothing but the One—
there is the Infinite.
Where one sees another, hears another, knows another—
there is the finite.
The Infinite is immortal, the finite is mortal.
It is written, He who has realized eternal Truth
does not see death, nor illness, nor pain;
he sees everything as the Self, and obtains all.

Chandogya Upanishad

What is important is the evidence gathered from various traditions that the mystic states are not delusional but further stages of spiritual development. Science, which, as mentioned earlier, restricts itself to a "what is true is what can be measured" rule, has difficulty recognizing stages beyond the egoic. In some ways the Sensitive stage, with its reintegration of the body into the self, can seem like a regression to an earlier stage when the body and the self were not yet differentiated. But there is a real and profound difference between them.

Given science's flat view of things, it is unable to distinguish between an institutionalized schizophrenic and a fully realized mystic. Both see visions and hear voices—that's what they share in common, that is what separates them from "normal" people. But St. Teresa of Avila was able to not only have and absorb these experiences, she was also able to keep herself out of the clutches of the Inquisition and to reform her religious order. The average institutionalized schizophrenic can't shop for groceries on their own.

The experiences of mystics across traditions and cultures point to real structures of consciousness in the future for most of us, and to which we are all called. The road of meditation is our way to follow these structures (the ox) into the future and toward the God who waits to welcome us home.

There is that in me—I do not know what it is
—but I know it is in me. . .
I do not know it—it is without name—it is a word
unsaid,
It is not in any dictionary, utterance, symbol. . .
Do you see O my brothers and sisters?
It is not chaos or death—it is form, union, plan—it is
eternal life—
it is Happiness.

Walt Whitman, Leaves of Grass

Glossary

Abishiktananda. A Christian monk who immigrated to India and bridged Hinduism and Christianity. See: *Prayer* (Westminster John Knox Press, 1973).

Abraham Isaak Kook. Jewish Kabballist Author. See: *The Lights of Penitence, Lights of Holiness: The Moral Principles, Essays, Letters and Poems* (Paulist Press, 1978).

acupressure, acupuncture points. Chinese medicine works upon the points along which energy (*chi*) flows throughout the body. Acupressure uses touch, acupuncture uses needles, and both are designed to balance the energies and promote health. See Web: http://www.letusreason.org/Nam10.htm

Adi Granth. See **Sikhism**

alleluia. Jewish and Christian mantra that means "Praise God."

American Yoga Association. The major resource for finding yoga teachings in the United States. Web site: http://www.americanyogaassociation.org/

asana. In yoga, the word for posture, such as a cobra asana or the corpse asana.

Baal Shem Tov. One of the great Jewish mystics and hasidim, 1698–1760. Many stories were told by him and about him. See Web: http://www.baalshemtov.com

Baba Ram Dass. Former Harvard psychologist who with colleague Timothy Leary sparked the psychedelic drug revival of the 1960s. After being fired from Harvard, he went to India to study and assumed his current name. He has gone on to do work in death and dying and caring for the dying. Best known work: *Be Here Now* (Crown Pub,1971). See also *Journey of Awakening : A Meditator's Guidebook* (Bantam Books, 1978).

Baptism. The Christian sacrament of initiation. It is either a total immersion in water or a sprinkling of water on the forehead.

Bhagavad Gita. A section of the great epic *The Mahabharata* of India, which has become the Hindu equivalent to the Christian gospels. Suggested version: *The Bhagavad Gita According to Gandhi* (Berkeley Hills Books, 2000).

Bhagwan Shree Rajneesh. A controversial Hindu guru who came to the United States and founded an *ashram* in Eastern Oregon. He was deported and has since died. In spite of the controversy, his books have much to offer the spiritual seeker. His current name is OSHO. See: *Meditation: The First and Last Freedom* (St. Martin's Press, 1997).

bhakti yoga. Yoga of devotion seen today in the Hare Krishna movement, in which the devotees repeatedly chant the name of Krishna.

Boddhisattva. In Mahayana Buddhism, a person who makes a vow not to enter nirvana until all sentient beings are enlightened.

Bodhi tree. The tree under which Buddha achieved enlightenment.

Brahman. The Hindu concept of the Ultimate Reality or God. Also the name of the chief God.

Buddha. See **Buddhism**

Buddha nature. In Mahayana Buddhism, the belief that states that the essence of each being is empty and therefore is the same as Buddha—empty of all being. Especially important in Zen and in some forms of Tibetan Buddhism.

Buddhism. The various schools that claim to follow the teachings of Gautama the Buddha, who lived in the fifth century B.C.E. and taught liberation from suffering. See Web: http://buddhism.about.com/

calm and clearing. see **Vipassana**

Campbell, Joseph. A popular modern teacher of mythology. See: *Hero With a Thousand Faces*

(Reprint, Princeton UP, 1972). With Bill Moyers, Campbell produced a series of videos available today. See Web: http://www.jcf.org/

Centering Prayer. A Christian form of meditation that is popular today and takes its inspiration from the medieval classic *The Cloud of Unknowing.* See: *Where Only Love Can Go: A Journey of the Soul into the Cloud of Unknowing* by John Kirvan (Ave Maria Press, 1996), and *The Cloud of Unknowing,* William Johnston (Image Books, Doubleday, 1973).

chakra. In Hinduism and Buddhism, refers to centers of spiritual energy, equivalent to pressure points in Chinese traditions.

Chan. Chinese term for Zen meditation.

Chesterton, G. K. Twentieth century English author who wrote in defense of Catholicism. Also author of the popular Fr. Brown mysteries.

chi. Chinese term for spiritual energy. See **prana**, etc. In Taoism, the student learns to manipulate the chi for health and fitness. See the meditation, Circulating the Chi, on page 139. See Mantak Chia's *Awaken Healing Energy Through the Tao* (Aurora Press, 1991).

Christianity. The religion founded on the teachings and example of Jesus of Nazareth, whom followers believe is the Christ, the Son of God, and savior.

Main branches: Orthodoxy, Catholicism, Protestantism. See Web: http://www.religioustolerance.org/christ.htm

circumcision. The removal of the sheath covering the tip of the male penis. Practiced in some religions, particularly **Judaism** and **Islam**.

Commandments. See **Ten Commandments.**

Confucianism. The religion that claims the Chinese sage Confucius as its founder. Especially concerned with ethics and the Good Life. See Web: http://www.askasia.org/frclasrm/readings/r000004.htm

crucifix. Christian symbol of Jesus Christ nailed to a cross. Minus the body it is known simply as a cross.

Cox, Harvey. Contemporary Protestant theologian who has been very active in interreligious dialogue. See: *Many Mansions: A Christian's Encounter With Other Faiths* (Beacon Press, 1988) and *Common Prayers: Faith, Family, and a Christian's Journey Through the Jewish Year* (Mariner Books, 2002). Also see *Turning East* (Simon & Schuster, 1978).

cult. A closed community that puts all its energy into following its spiritual way. A cult generates tremendous energy to bring to the practice, but it does so at the expense of individual freedom.

Dante. Christian Italian medieval poet who wrote the *Divine Comedy,* an epic poem describing his journey through Hell, Purgatory, and Heaven. See: *The Inferno of Dante: A New Verse Translation,* Bilingual edition (Noonday Press, 1996).

deadly sins, (seven). Medieval Christian list of the root sins, which cause all others: Sloth, Anger, Pride, Envy, Avarice, Gluttony, and Lust.

Dependent Origination. Buddhist teaching demonstrating how all things are interrelated. Goes by various names. See Web: http://www.chezpaul.org.uk/buddhism/books/wheel/depend.htm

dharma, dhamma. Buddhist term refers to 1) the Truth or teaching of the Buddha, 2) in plural, teachings, and 3) basic elements of existence.

Divine Comedy. see **Dante.**

Donne, John. English Christian preacher and poet who lived in the seventeenth century.

Easter. Most important Christian feast celebrating Jesus' Resurrection from the dead. Occurs in the Spring.

Ego. Greek and Latin word for I. Used by spirituality and psychology to refer to that component of the psyche which stands for the I or the individual being.

Eightfold Path. The path to liberation set forth by the Buddha.

Eleusis. Ancient Greek shrine where pilgrims would journey for divine guidance.

esoteric. Refers to hidden or secret teaching. What is within.

exoteric. Refers to a religion's common or public teaching, which is available to everyone as opposed to esoteric teaching, which is hidden.

Ezekiel. Hebrew prophet whose visions are recounted in the biblical book bearing his name.

Four Noble Truths. Buddhist teachings of 1) suffering, 2) the cause of suffering, 3) the cure for suffering, and 4) the **Eightfold Path** (see).

Fox, George. One of the founders of the Christian Quaker movement and a major Protestant mystic. See Web: http://www.strecorsoc.org/gfox/title.html

fundamentalism. An Evangelical movement that began in late 19th century America in opposition to Protestant Liberalism and the secular world. Asserts the infallibility of Scripture.

Gandhi. Twentieth century Indian leader who led his people in throwing off British rule in India. Used nonviolence as his method.

Gentile. Jewish term for a non-Jew.

Griffiths, Bede. Catholic monk who has been a great inspiration in interreligious dialogue between

Christians and Hindus. At the end of his life he founded a Christian-Hindu Ashram in India which still exists. Books include: *A New Vision of Reality: Western Science, Eastern Mysticism and Christian Faith* (Templegate Pub, 1992).

Gurdjieff, George Ivanovich. Armenian-born spiritual teacher who claimed to have encountered the hidden wisdom of the ages. Founded the Institute for the Harmonious Development of Man in 1919. See: *Meetings With Remarkable Men* (E P Dutton, 1991).

guru. Sanskrit term for a spiritual master and teacher. Common in **Hinduism** and **Buddhism.**

Hadith. In Islam, the sayings of the prophet Mohammed collected by his followers. Holy writings but not considered equivalent with the Qur'an.

half lotus asana. See **lotus asana.**

Hare Krishna. See **bhakti yoga.**

Hassidism. A form of mystical Orthodox Judaism that began in the 1700s in Eastern Europe. It was founded by Rabbi Israel ben Eliezer, who is better known as the Baal Shem Tov (Besht for short), which means Master of the Good Name in Hebrew. See Web: http://www.pinenet.com/~rooster/hasid1.html

hatha yoga. The yoga of asanas and breathing.

Heart Sutra. Buddhist Scripture on the Perfection of Wisdom. Particularly important in Zen. See Web: http://members.ozemail.com.au/~mooncharts/heart sutra/english.html

Hell. The state in which the damned suffer after death. Common in many religions.

Hinayana. The lesser vehicle of early Buddhism. Revealed the **Four Noble Truths** and the **Eightfold Path.**

Hinduism. The religious traditions of the Indian subcontinent, which are not part of Buddhism. Jainism, or other religious traditions such as Islam or Christianity. See Web: http://www.geocities.com/RodeoDrive/1415/indexd.html

Holy Spirit. The third Person of the Trinity in Christianity. Similar to **ruach.**

Huxley, Aldous. Modern philosopher and novelist. Best known novel: *Brave New World.* Experimented with psychedelic drugs. Helped revive his philosophy with his book *The Perennial Philosophy,* (reprint Harper Collins, 1990). These teachings are found in all the great spiritual traditions. Includes the concept of the Great Chain of Being.

incarnation. Becoming flesh. A term common to Christianity and Hinduism as well as other traditions. The Christian doctrine refers to the Second Person of the Godhead taking human form in Jesus.

initiation. The process by which a disciple is welcomed into a tradition. In Christianity it is baptism, in Buddhism it is taking refuge.

Insight Meditation. See **Vipassana.**

Integral Psychology. See **Wilbur, Ken.**

Isherwood, Christopher. Twentieth century author who helped introduce Vedanta to the West. See: *My Guru and His Disciples,* (reprint, University of Minnesota Press, 2001).

Islam. Religious tradition that follows the Qur'an as the voice of God and the teachings of Mohammed his prophet, who lived in the sixth century C.E. See Web: http://www.islamworld.net/

Iyengar. Popular Yoga teacher who has established himself in the West. Perhaps the most popular form of yoga in the West today. See Web site: http://www.bksiyengar.com/

Jesus. See **Christianity.**

Jesus Prayer. Eastern Christian form of meditation, which focuses upon the name of Jesus. It became popular in the West through the small classic *The Way of a Pilgrim* (see: trans. R. M. French, reprint, HarperSanFrancisco, 1991.) Mentioned in J. D.

Salinger's novel, *Franey and Zooey.* The classic Greek collected writings on the Jesus Prayer are found in the multi-volumed *Philokalia.* Eds. G. E. Palmer, Kallistos T. Ware (Philip Sherrard Faber & Faber, 1986).

jnana yoga. A discipline of knowledge and the study of philosophy.

Jubu. Slang modern term for a Jewish Buddhist. See the Web site http://www.innerjew.com/index.html for an interesting discussion of the relation between meditation and specific spiritual traditions with the focus on Judaism.

Judaism. The faith of the Jewish people going back to Abraham and Moses. See Web: http://judaism.about.com/

Kabbala. The esoteric teachings of the Jewish faith. See Web: http://www.kabbalah.info/

Kakuan Shion. See **Ox Herding Pictures.**

karma yoga. Yoga of work.

kensho. Zen Buddhist term for a brief glimpse of reality, a taste of nirvana. But the person has far to travel to total enlightenment. See **satori.**

King, Jr., Dr. Martin Luther. Baptist Minister who in the 1950s and 1960s led the African American struggle for Civil Rights in the United States.

Kingdom of God. Jesus' term for the reality he preached and inaugurated.

koan. Zen Buddhist term for a short puzzle used to break through to a new way of seeing.

Kornfield, Jack. A popular American Buddhist meditation teacher. See: *A Path with Heart: A Guide Through the Perils and Promises of Spiritual Life* (Bantam Doubleday Dell, 1993). See Web: http://www.spiritwalk.org/kornfield.htm

Krishnamurti. Modern Hindu spiritual teacher popular in the West. See: *Total Freedom: The Essential Krishnamurti* (Harper San Francisco, 1996). See Web: http://www.kfa.org/

Kum Nye Relaxation. A system of body meditation designed by the Tibetan Buddhist guru Tarthang Tulku Rimpoche to help Westerns ground in their bodies. See Tarthang Tulku's *Kum Nye Relaxation* 2 vols. (Dharma Publishing, 1979).

lotus asana. The traditional Asian meditation posture. The **half lotus** is a simplified posture more suitable to Westerners.

Maharishi Mahesh Yogi. Hindu teacher who founded Transcendental Meditation Movement. See Web: http://www.tm.org/

Mahayana. Buddhist term for the Greater Vehicle, which reveals the teachings of emptiness and the Buddha

Nature. The major form of Buddhism in the world today.

mala. Hindu and Buddhist term for a strand of prayer beads.

Mansur al-Halaj. Tenth century Persian Sufi.

mantra. Sanskrit term for a syllable or phrase used as a basis for meditation.

martial arts. Collection of various Asian disciplines that use spiritual energy to develop the body and mind for combat and spiritual growth. Examples are Tai Chi Chuan, judo, karate, and Tai Kwan Do.

Maslow, Abraham. One of the founders of Third Force Psychology (also known as Transpersonal Psychology), which studies phenomenon beyond the ego. Coined the term "Peak Experiences." See: *Religious Values and Peak Experiences.* (Viking Press, 1994).

McKenna, Terrence. American teacher who believed that psychedelic drugs played and could still play a part in the evolution of human consciousness. See: *The Invisible Landscape: Mind, Hallucinogens, and the I Ching* (1975; reprint, Harper San Francisco, 1994). See Web: http://www.telesterion.com/esoteric books/terrence.htm and http://www.deoxy.org/mckenna.htm

medicine man. See **shaman.**

Meister Eckhart. Christian medieval mystic who is emerging today as bridge between Christianity and Buddhism. He has never been condemned by the Western Church but has until recently suffered under a cloud of suspicion. See: *God Awaits You: Based on the Classic Spirituality of Meister Eckhart,* Ed. Richard Chilson (Ave Maria Press, 1996).

metta. Pali term for compassion in **Theravada** Buddhism.

Milarepa. One of the greatest Tibetan Buddhists and founder of a major Tibetan school. He is also a great poet. The exemplar of the Buddhist way. Equivalent in Tibet to St. Francis of Assisi in the West. See Web: http://www.c-level.com/milarepa/

monastery. A place where a group of monks or nuns lives. Implies a life of common prayer, work, and study.

Moulana Shah Maghsoud. Twentieth Century Persian Sufi.

mudra. Sanskrit term for a hand gesture, which a person assumes in meditation.

mystics. People who have insights into the beyond. These experiences may be induced or spontaneous. Found in all cultures and colored by the religious and spiritual traditions of the person.

Nagarjuna. Buddhist founder (c. 200 B.C.E.–200 C.E.) of the **Mahayana** Vehicle. He is said to have discovered the Mahayana Scriptures. He also developed the Madhyamika philosophy of sunyata or openness, which is the foundation of the Mahayana. See Web: http://altzen.freeyellow.com/page9.html

nihilism. Philosophy which claims nothing exists; it is often confused with the Buddhist position that no self sustaining entity perdures.

nirvana. Buddhist term for the state of total enlightenment. Hard to translate, harder to understand because it transcends our ability to conceive and name. Sometime called extinction or bliss.

OM, OHM, AUM. Sanskrit holy syllable. Various spellings. Used by Buddhists and Hindus and thought to be the most sacred sound.

Orthodox Christianity. See **Christianity.**

OSHO. See **Bhagwan Shree Rajneesh.**

Ox Herding Pictures. Asian pictures (number varies) used to illustrate the meditative path. Originated by Kakuan Shion, a twelfth century *rinzai* zen master. Found in various Asian cultures and with different artists. See Web:http:// www.jaysquare.com/ljohnson/ox-herding.html

Padmasambhava. Magician and Guru who first brought the Buddhist teaching to Tibet (817 C.E.) Often referred to simply as Guru Rimpoche. See Web: http://www.muktinath.org/buddhism/ padmasambhava1.htm

Pali. An ancient variant of Sanskrit that became the sacred language of **Theravada** Buddhism. The Sanskrit Buddhist texts have not survived.

Paradise. The state people enter after death, in which they enjoy perfection and bliss. Found in a number of spiritual and religious traditions. Another term for heaven.

Paramahansa Yogananda. Hindu teacher who came to the United States in the mid twentieth century and founded the Self Realization Fellowship (see Web: http://www.yogananda-srf.org/). He taught many Westerners including **Christopher Isherwood** and **Aldous Huxley.** Also wrote the bestseller *Autobiography of a Yogi* (Self Realization Fellowship Pub., 1979).

Patanjali. Ancient Indian author who collected the sayings that have become the classical text for yoga commentaries. See: *How to Know God: The Yoga Aphorisms of Patanjali* (Vedanta Press, 1996). See Web: http://www.santosha.com/philosophy/yoga-sutras.html

penthius. Greek term in Christian Orthodoxy that describes the position of humility and repentance which a believer assumes before God.

Philokalia. See **Jesus Prayer.**

Platonist. Follower of the philosopher Plato, who claimed that ideas were the true ultimate and that everyday reality was but a pallid reflection of the real.

prana. Sanskrit term for breath, psychic, or spiritual energy.

Pravhavananda, Swami. A modern Hindu teacher. See: *The Sermon on the Mount According to Vedanta* (reissue New American Library, 1986), and *How to Know God: The Yoga Aphorisms of Patanjali* (Vedanta Press, 1996).

Prayer of the Name. See **Jesus Prayer.**

precepts (Buddhism). The five precepts a Buddhist accepts as the way to entering on the path: no killing, no sexual misconduct, no lying, no stealing, no intoxicants.

Principles (Islam). The basic code guiding a Muslim's behavior: daily prayers (*selat*), fasting (*sawm*), the pilgrimage (*hajj*) to Mecca, the religious tax (*zakat*), and holy struggle (*jihad*).

prophet. In Judeo-Christian tradition, a person called by God to speak truth to the nation. The Hebrew prophets did not foretell the future, but rather said that if people do not change, God would incur consequences.

Protestantism. See **Christianity.**

psalm. A song of praise in the Jewish and Christian traditions. Psalms is one book in the Bible.

psychedelic drugs. Psychedelic means mind revealing. Term applied to certain substances that have the power to open consciousness to transpersonal dimensions. Includes LSD (acid), psilocybin mushrooms, peyote, and others. Hallucinogens is another term having a derogatory meaning, implying that the substances merely cause hallucinations or delusions.

Pure Land. A **Mahayana** Buddhist school where a Buddha vows to liberate beings who come to him for refuge. They will be reborn in a Pure Land, where they will be able to devote themselves to meditation and achieve enlightenment. Probably the largest percent of Mahayana Buddhists today are some variant of Pure Land Buddhism.

Purgatory. In Catholicism, the intermediate state of the afterlife between heaven and hell. Here, souls are cleansed and purified of their sins before entering paradise.

rabbi. Jewish title for teacher.

Rabbi Nachman of Breslov. Rebbe Nachman of Breslov (1772–1810), a Hasidic leader in Ukraine during a turbulent time of religious persecution, avoided obscure religious references to any holy book while encouraging readers to "never despair!" and "get into the habit of dancing." "Always remember: Joy is not merely incidental to your spiritual quest, it is vital." See: *The Empty Chair: Finding Hope & Joy—Timeless Wisdom From a Hasidic Master*, Ed. Moshe Mykof (Jewish Lights Pub., 1996).

raja yoga. Yoga of meditation.

refuge. The way of becoming a Buddhist. "I take refuge in the Buddha, the Dharma, and the Sangha."

resurrection. Belief that the body will rise after death to new life. Christians believe this has already happened to Jesus and will happen to all at the end of the world.

retreat. A term referring to a time set aside for intensive meditation practice—a weekend, a week, or longer. It often takes place at a monastery or retreat house.

Rinzai Zen. School of Zen Buddhism which uses the **koan** for practice.

Rosary. Term from the Catholic tradition. A strand of beads with which prayers are said. Found in many different traditions with various names. See **mala.**

ruach, ruh. Hebrew and Arabic terms for Holy Spirit.

Rumi. Mowlana Jalaluddin Rumi (1207–1273), great Sufi poet. Said to be the most read poet in America today. See: *The Essential Rumi,* Ed. Coleman Barks (Harper San Francisco, 1997). See Web: http://www.khamush.com/

Sabbath. A day set aside for rest, prayer, and worship in the Jewish and Christian traditions. Jews keep Saturday while Christians keep Sunday, in honor of the Resurrection.

Sacrament. In Catholicism and the Orthodox Church the seven basic rituals by which one encounters God in one's life: Baptism, Confirmation, Eucharist, Penance, Anointing of the Sick, Marriage, and Holy Orders. Protestants as a whole only acknowledge Baptism and Eucharist and may have different understandings of the rituals.

Salute to the Sun. A basic routine of **asanas** from **hatha yoga.**

samsara. Buddhist term for ordinary existence as opposed to **nirvana.**

samatha. See **Vipassana.**

sangha. Buddhist term for the community. In a narrow sense it refers to monks and nuns but more broadly refers to all who have taken refuge.

Sanskrit. Medieval Indian language in which the **Vedas, Upanishad,** and other scriptures are written. It is part of the Indo-European family of languages.

satori. Zen Buddhist term for enlightenment.

Secret of the Golden Flower. A Taoist Classic on meditation. Through the practice the mind becomes attuned to reality in a way that inhibits the degeneration of consciousness and begins to restore the life of the heart and soul. See *Secret of the Golden Flower,* Trans. Thomas Cleary (reprint, Harper San Francisco, 1993).

secular spiritualities. Refers to spiritualities which are not connected with any specific religious tradition, such as Alcoholics Anonymous or Herbert Benson's Relaxation Response.

sesshin. Zen Buddhist term for an intensive meditation retreat. It is not uncommon to spend eighteen hours a day in meditation, sitting and walking.

shaman. A person in a primal culture who has undergone training and had special experience in the spiritual arts and who ministers to his people. Sometimes called a Medicine man or woman.

Shariputra. The Buddha's disciple, who received the **sutras** (texts of teachings).

Shingon. Japanese form of tantric Buddhism. See Web: http://www.shingon.org/

Siddharta, Gautama. The Indian prince who is the human form of the **Buddha** (see) in the present age. As crucial to Buddhism as Christ is for Christians.

Sikhism. A blending of **Hinduism** and **Islam** founded more than five hundred years ago. The Scriptures of the Sikhs are known as the *Adi Granth.* See Web: http://www.sikhs.org/

Silk Road. The ancient trading route between the West and the East in the first centuries C.E. It extended between Ephesis in modern Turkey all the way to China, and was influential in distributing information between these civilizations.

sloth. One of the seven deadly sins. It is nonattention to essentials and is similar to laziness.

Socrates. Ancient Greek teacher who taught by asking his disciples questions. He did not write himself but his greatest student, Plato, passed on his tradition as did Plato's greatest student, Aristotle.

soma. Sanskrit term for the nectar of the gods, an ancient potion that provided enlightenment and happiness.

Soto Zen. School of Japanese Zen Buddhism, which centers around sitting meditation. See Web: http://www.pa.airnet.ne.jp/szi/

spiritual centers. See **chakras.**

Spiritual Exercises. See **St. Ignatius of Loyola.**

Sri Aurobindo. Modern Hindu teacher who sought to synthesize the Indian traditions. Had a great devotion to the mother whom he believed incarnated in an Indian woman who was left to carry on his legacy. See: *Integral Yoga: Sri Aurobindo's Teaching & Method of Practice* (Lotus Press, 1998). See Web: http://www.sriaurobindosociety.org.in/index.htm

St. Athanasius. Eastern Doctor of the Church and a primary architect of Christian tradition. Saved the church from the Arian heresy. Taught that in Jesus, God became man so that through Jesus man might become God. This gives rise to the idea of theosis or divinization in Orthodox Christianity. Western Christianity prefers the term sanctification.

St. Dominic. Medieval Christian founder of the Dominicans who promoted the Rosary to help revive the faith. Contemporary of St. Francis of Assisi.

St. Francis of Assisi. Medieval Christian mystic inspired the first Renaissance in Europe and founded the Franciscan order. He followed God by following Lady Poverty.

St. Ignatius of Loyola. Counter Reformation Catholic and founder of the Jesuit order. He trained his men in a form of meditation described in the Spiritual

Exercises. Today many Catholics follow his spiritual path. See Web: http://www.ccel.org/i/ignatius/exercises/exercises.html

St. John of the Cross. A medieval Catholic mystic now considered a Doctor of the Church as is **St. Teresa of Avila.** Founders and reformers of the Carmelite religious orders. See: *The Collected Works of Saint John of the Cross,* trans. Kieran Kavanaugh (Rev. ed. ICS Pub., 2001), and *Collected Works of Saint Teresa of Avila,* 3 vols. (ICS Pub., 1976).

St. Paul. Most important author of the New Testament books. He shaped the Christian teaching and after Jesus himself is widely considered to be the most important former of the Christian religion.

St. Teresa of Avila. See **St. John of the Cross.**

Steindl-Rast, David. A current Christian spiritual teacher. See his books: *Living Buddha, Living Christ With Thich Nhat Hanh* (Riverhead Books, 1997), and *A Listening Heart: The Spirituality of Sacred Sensuousness,* rev. ed. (Crossroad/Herder & Herder, 1999).

stopping and seeing. See **Vipassana.**

Sufism. Refers to the various mystical schools of Islam. The students are known as Sufis. The most famous Sufi is the poet Rumi.

sunyata. The key concept of **Mahayana** Buddhism: everything is impermanent, without self, open, empty. Does not mean it doesn't exist but that it is perduring.

sutra, sutta. Buddhist term for a book of scripture.

Suzuki, Shunnyu. Japanese Buddhist teacher influential in bringing Buddhism to the United States. See: *Zen Mind, Beginner's Mind* (Weatherhill, 1997).

Tai Chi Chih. Simplified form of Tai Chi developed by the American Justin Stone. See: Justin Stone, *Tai Chi Chih! Joy Through Movement* (Good Karma Press, 1996).

Tai Chi Chuan. The most ancient martial art and mother to all the others. More related today to meditation than to fighting.

Taizé. Contemporary Christian ecumenical monastery in France. A great force in the current ecumenical movement and the renewal of Christian meditation and spirituality.

tantra. Sanskrit term for various disciplines which help the practitioner advance quickly upon a spiritual path. Common to both Hinduism and Buddhism. Not a new teaching as such but rather new techniques and practices.

Tao Te Ching. Primary scripture of Taoism traced back to the Taoist Immortal Lao Tse. See: *The Essential Tao:*

An Initiation into the Heart of Taoism Through the Authentic Tao Te Ching and the Inner Teachings of Chuang-Tzu, trans. Thomas Cleary (reprint. HarperSanFrancisco, 1993).

Taoism. Describes Chinese traditions stemming from the Seven Immortals. Has various forms today including both the philosophical and magic degenerative forms. See Web: http://www.clas.ufl.edu/users/gthursby/taoism/intros.htm

Tarthang Tulku. Tibetan Buddhist guru and founder of the Nyingma Institute in the West, which expounds the teachings of the Nyingma—the Old School—of Tibetan Buddhism. See: *Gesture of Balance* (Dharma Publishing, 1977). See also Web: http://www.nyingma.org/

Temple (Hebrew). The center of worship for the Hebrew people in Jerusalem until its destruction in 70 C.E. This destruction resulted in the formation of both Rabbinic Judaism and Christianity. Today a Jewish place of worship may still be called a temple but it is not to be confused with the Temple in Jerusalem whose restoration is still hoped for. The common name for a Jewish place of worship today is the synagogue.

Ten Commandments. Core of the Law given by God to Moses and Israel for Jews and retained by Christians.

Theravada. Form of Buddhism found today in South Asia except Vietnam. Refers to the "Way of the Elders." Not the same as **Hinayana.** Promotes **Vipassana** meditation.

Thich Nhat Hanh. Contemporary Vietnamese Buddhist teacher popular in the West. See: *Miracle of Mindfulness* (Beacon Press, 1999). See also: *Being Peace* (Parallax Press, 1988), and *Going Home: Jesus and Buddha As Brothers* (Riverhead Books, 2000).

Thomas à Kempis. Medieval author of the Christian spiritual classic *Imitation of Christ.* See: John Kirvan's *True Serenity: Based on Thomas à Kempis's the Imitation of Christ* (Ave Maria Press, 1995).

Torah. The first five books of the Old Testament (Genesis, Exodus, Leviticus, Numbers, and Deutoronomy.)

Transcendental Meditation (TM). Form of meditation developed by Maharishi Mahesh Yogi, which uses a secret mantra as its focus. See Web: http://www.tm.org/

Upanishad. The "New Testament" scriptures of **Hinduism.** The **Vedas** are the equivalent of the Old Testament. They expound the various philosophies of the Indian tradition. The Upanishads are expositions of doctrine, typically found in the concluding portions of the Brahmanas and Aranyakas of the four Vedas. A number of Upanishads are extant today, with commentaries on them by representatives of various schools of Vedanta. The Upanishads are not to be seen as uniform books—each text is connected to the Veda in which it occurs, and the upanishadic teaching is often presented in the context of a particular vedic hymn or ritual.

Vajrayana. The Diamond Vehicle in Tibetan Buddhism. Refers to Tantric Buddhism. No new philosophy, rather new techniques.

Vedanta. Sanskrit term for the major philosophical form of Hindu philosophy today. Developed by Shankara and taught by most modern Hindu teachers. It is a nondual philosophy and bears many resemblances to Buddhist philosophy, which influenced it. See Web: http://www.advaita-vedanta.org/avhp/

Vedas. The most ancient scriptures of the Indian subcontinent. Acceptance of them can define one as a Hindu, but few Hindus actually read them. There are four Vedas, the Rig Veda, Sama Veda, Yajur Veda, and Atharva Veda. They also had a vast influence on **Buddhism,** Jainism, and **Sikhism.** See Web: http://www.sacred-texts.com/hin/

view (Buddhist). The particular view one follows along the spiritual path. One also has a path and this leads to fruits.

Vipassana. Means "to see things as they really are." It is the most common form of Buddhist Meditation. Often called Insight Meditation. Names may vary. Buddhist terms for the complete basic practice of meditation, also known as stopping and seeing and calm and clearing. Actually composed of two practices: Samatha and Vipassana. Samatha is called stopping, or calming. It involves slowing down the mind and developing concentration. Vipassana refers to seeing or clearing. It focuses the mind on the passing stream of thoughts etc. See Web: http://www.dhamma.org/ and http://www.dhamma.org/vipassan.htm

vision quest. Native American term for the spiritual journey a young male makes to encounter the invisible world, be transformed, and bring back gifts for the community.

visualization. A series of meditation techniques that use the imagination.

Way of the Pilgrim. See Jesus Prayer.

Weil, Andrew. Graduated from Harvard with an M.D. but has never practiced traditional medicine. Has written on drugs and the need to get high. Wrote *The Natural Mind: A New Way of Looking at Drugs* *and the Higher Consciousness* (rev. ed., Houghton Mifflin, 1998), and *From Chocolate to Morphine: Everything You Need to Know About Mind-Altering Drugs* (rev. ed., Houghton Mifflin, 1993). He is currently best known as a health advisor. See Web: http://www.drweil.com/app/cda/drw_cda.html

Whitman, Walt. American poet and mystic. His best-known work is *Leaves of Grass.*

Wilbur, Ken. Modern writer who is creating a contemporary spiritual synthesis. He calls his work Integral Psychology. A brief summary of his work so far appears in *A Short History of Everything* (Shambala Publications, 2001). This book is in turn a summary of his major work to date: *Sex, Ecology and Spirituality* (Shambala Publications, 1995). See Web: http://wilber.shambhala.com/

yoga. Sanskrit term for yoke. To join the physical, emotional, mental, and spiritual dimensions together. Takes many forms of which **hatha yoga** is the most familiar.

zafu. Zen meditation cushion.

Zen. Japanese for meditation. Refers to a branch of Buddhism found in East Asia that focuses on meditation.

RICHARD W. CHILSON is a member of the Paulists currently engaged in retreat ministry. His home base is Portland, but he travels widely. He is the author of numerous books, among them *Yeshua of Nazareth: Spiritual Master* , three of the *Thirty Days with a Great Spiritual Teacher* series: *All Will Be Well* (Julian of Norwich), *God Awaits You* (Meister Eckhart), and *You Shall Not Want* (The Psalms), and various titles for Paulist Press, including the best seller *Catholic Christianity: A Guide to the Way, the Truth, and the Life.*